CALLED TO SONSHIP
Getting Free from an Orphan Heart

Christopher Kenneth Turney

Scripture quotations appear by permission as follows:

Scripture quotations marked (NKJV) are taken from the New King James Version®. Copyright © 1982 by Thomas Nelson. Used by permission. All rights reserved.

Scripture quotations marked (NIV) are taken from the Holy Bible, New International Version®, NIV®. Copyright © 1973, 1978, 1984, 2011 by Biblica, Inc.™ Used by permission. All rights reserved worldwide.

Scripture quotations marked (ESV) are from The Holy Bible, English Standard Version®. Copyright © 2001 by Crossway, a publishing ministry of Good News Publishers. Used by permission. All rights reserved

ISBN: 979-8-218-80450-3 (paperback)
ISBN: 979-8-218-80556-2 (hard cover)

Acknowledgments

I want to extend my heartfelt thanks to those who have walked with me on the path of sonship. To my wife Jill, your strength and love have been an anchor. You've pointed my life into the Father's arms. To my mother, whose enduring spirit and prayers laid a foundation of faith and hope in my life. To Bishop Gary and Pastor Lydia Clowers, thank you for your unwavering support, spiritual example, and love.

To all my children my life is the best it could be being your father. I love you all so much.

To the Kingdom Reign Ministries family, you have been more than a church. You are sons, daughters, and co-laborers in this journey. Thank you for your hunger, your trust, and your pursuit of the Father's heart.

To every spiritual son and daughter reading this, this is for you. May you rise, walk in your identity, and father the next generation with a healed heart and holy fire.

And finally, to Abba Father, thank You for calling me a son. Thank You for not giving up on me even when I had given up on myself. May this book glorify You and point others home.

Table of Contents

FOREWORD

Two weeks before my father, Gerald Kennedy, passed away on 1 October 2002, he looked me in the eye and asked a question I'll never forget:

"Who told Adam that he was naked?"

With the depth and weight of a father's wisdom, he added, "You and the church don't get it."

For over two decades, that moment has echoed in my spirit. I've watched, prayed, and listened as the revelation of sonship has steadily gained momentum in the body of Christ. And now, 23 years later, I believe I've found a voice that not only understands the question but carries the answer.

Apostle Chris Turney delivers a profound, Spirit-breathed work in this book. His ability to distill deep truths into single, piercing sentences is remarkable. These insights don't just teach; they transform. Each quote, each chapter, is a tool to help shape ordinary Christians into sons who know who they are and whose they are.

I wish my father could read this. Because now, I can finally say: *"There is someone in Port Saint Lucie, Florida who gets it."*

Andrew Kennedy
Cornerstone Church
Middelburg, South Africa

PREFACE

I never set out to write a book about sonship. In fact, for much of my life, I didn't even understand what it meant to be a son, at least not in the way the Father intended.

When I lost my earthly father at the age of twelve, something in me shifted. I became strong too early. I became responsible too soon. I lived with the sense that if anything was going to get done, I had to be the one to do it. That inner vow followed me into manhood, into ministry, and into leadership. I took care of others. I showed up for people. But beneath the outward call was an inward ache, an ache for belonging, for rest, for identity. I was serving God, but I didn't know how to simply be with Him.

Over the years, God began to unravel my performance and reintroduce me to His love. He sent a spiritual father into my life. He dismantled my orphan thinking. He reminded me that before I was a preacher, I was a son. Before I ever carried a burden, He carried me.

This book is not just theological, it's deeply personal. It is born out of prayer, tears, revelation, and years of walking the long road home to the Father's heart. It is a call, not to strive harder, but to surrender deeper. A call to stop performing and start receiving. A call to remember that the Father is not building institutions, but a family. And that family is made up of sons and daughters who reflect His nature in the earth.

Called to Sonship is for the weary servant, the striving leader, and the orphan-hearted child. It's for anyone who has ever questioned their worth or wondered if they belong. My prayer is that as you read these pages, the voice of the Father would rise above every other voice, and you would hear Him say, "You are My beloved child, in whom I am well pleased."

Welcome home.

Christopher Turney
Kingdom Reign Ministries

INTRODUCTION
THE JOURNEY HOME

This book was never meant to be a manual, it's a map back home. Not to a house of religion, but to the Father's heart. Not to performance, but to presence. Not to hierarchy, but to inheritance.

I didn't write 'Called to Sonship' because I had it all figured out. I wrote it because I lived for too long as a spiritual orphan, saved, anointed, even used by God... but still unsure if I truly belonged. I knew how to preach, but not always how to receive. I knew how to lead, but I hadn't learned how to be fathered.

Many believers today are in the same place. They call God "Father" but serve Him like slaves. They build ministries and pursue success, but their inner life remains marked by fear, rejection, and striving. They are redeemed, but not yet rooted.

But the Gospel was never just about saving sinners. It was always about revealing sons.

The message of 'Called to Sonship' is simple but transformative:

You were not merely rescued, you were received.

You are not a servant, you are a beloved heir.

You were not born to survive, you were born to reign.

In these pages, we will walk through the identity, formation, and manifestation of sons. We will uncover the orphan mindset and replace it with Kingdom reality. We will confront the lie that worth is earned, and rediscover the truth that love is inherited.

Whether you are a pastor, a parent, a leader, or a new believer, this journey is for you. Because until you know the Father, you cannot reflect Him. And until you become a son, you cannot raise sons.

Let this book be your invitation to return, not just to doctrine, but to the embrace of Abba.
Let it restore your dignity, reframe your calling, and release your legacy.

The Father is not waiting for you to do something.
He's waiting for you to be someone…His son.

CHAPTER 1
THE FIRST SON

Built as a son, Called as a son

"...Adam, the son of God." — Luke 3:38 (NKJV)

Though God revealed Himself as Creator to all, He revealed Himself as Father to man.

While the heavens declare His glory and the earth displays His craftsmanship, only man was formed in His image and likeness. All creation knew His power, but Adam knew His breath. In creating everything else, God showed what He could do. But in forming man, He revealed who He is, a Father.

This distinction sets the tone for all of Scripture. While the rest of creation was spoken into being, man was formed and breathed into, marking him not just as a creature, but as a son.

And it is this very revelation, God as Father, that Jesus reintroduces at the outset of His ministry. He didn't begin with miracles or declarations of judgment. He began with a relational restoration:

"When you pray, say: Our Father…" (Luke 11:2, NKJV)

Jesus wasn't offering a new title, He was unveiling the original relationship, the one Adam once walked in but lost sight of. His entire redemptive mission was not just to forgive sin but to restore sonship, reconnecting us with the Father's house, the Father's voice, and the Father's likeness.

The Gospel is not just about saving sinners, it's about calling sons.

Before He was called Lord, before He was worshiped as Almighty, God revealed Himself through the one He made, and the one He made was a son. Adam was not merely the first man; he was the first son.

Though Adam was built and not born, he was created with all the intentionality, affection, and likeness of a Father forming His child. Genesis 1:26 reveals the divine blueprint:

"Then God said, 'Let Us make man in Our image, according to Our likeness..." (Genesis 1:26, NKJV)

This was not just an act of creation, it was an act of reproduction. God transferred something of Himself into Adam, not just functionality, but identity.

The Image and Likeness Are Relational, Not Just Representational

"When Adam had lived 130 years, he had a son in his own likeness, in his own image; and he named him Seth." (Genesis 5:3, NIV)

The repetition of 'image' and 'likeness' in both God's creation of Adam and Adam's begetting of Seth confirms something profound: image and likeness imply sonship. This is not about physical resemblance, it's about relational origin and authority.

Just as Seth was Adam's son, Adam was God's. And when God called to Adam in the garden (Genesis 3:9), He didn't say, 'Sinner, where are you?' He said: "Adam, where are you?" (NKJV)

He was calling to identity, not labeling failure. Even in Adam's fall, God addressed him as a son, not a criminal.

But the Lord recently showed me something deeper about the fall, something I had not seen before.

When the serpent spoke to Eve, he told her two things: *"You shall not surely die"* (Genesis 3:4) a lie, and *"For God knows that in the day you eat of it, your eyes will be opened, and you will be like God, knowing good and evil"* (Genesis 3:5) a truth.

This is how deception works. It starts with a lie and wraps it in enough truth to make it believable.

The root was false, *"you shall not surely die"* but what followed was accurate. Their eyes were opened. They did become aware of good and evil. But because they didn't drop dead on the spot, the lie seemed to become experientially true. In that moment, the serpent's deception became more believable than the word of the Lord. Their experience now appeared to affirm the lie.

And that's still how the enemy works today.

He will feed us lies that our experiences appear to validate.

You're not loved.

You're worthless.

You'll never be enough.

And if people treat us poorly... if we're abandoned, abused, or overlooked... it becomes easier to believe the lie than the word of the Lord.

But truth is not based on experience, it is rooted in the Word of God. We must not believe what our experience affirms if it contradicts what the Father has said. And this brings us to one of the most overlooked truths in Genesis 3.

God did not remove Adam and Eve from the Garden because He was angry or vindictive. He did it to protect them from reinforcing the lie.

He said:

"Lest he put out his hand and take also of the tree of life, and eat, and live forever" (Genesis 3:22, NKJV).

Had they remained in the Garden and continued eating from the tree of life after disobeying God, they would have wrongly assumed:

"See? The serpent was right. We didn't die. We're still alive. We can keep living forever."

In love, the Father interrupted the false narrative. He removed them from the Garden to uphold the truth of His word, *"in the day you eat of it, you shall surely die."*

The removal was not punishment. It was mercy.

It was the Father's intervention to prevent them from reinforcing a deception that would bury their identity even deeper under shame.

Even in judgment, God's motive was love.

Even in discipline, He was still Father.

Likeness, Image, and the Pattern for Kingdom Colonization

God's plan was never simply to populate the earth with people. His intention was to colonize the earth with His likeness, sons and daughters who carry His nature, reflect His rule, and walk in His authority.

"Then God said, 'Let Us make man in Our image, according to Our likeness; let them have dominion…" (Genesis 1:26, NKJV)

Image and likeness are not just decorative terms, they are governmental ones. Man was created to represent Heaven's order on earth. Dominion was tied to design: God's sons would be His agents of influence, His royal representatives. Sonship was always the strategy for colonization.

Divided to Multiply: The Wisdom of Divine Division

Though Adam was one, he carried within him the full capacity for legacy. But legacy cannot come from singularity. What was whole had to be divided in order to multiply. So even after declaring creation 'very good,' God said:

"It is not good that man should be alone…" (Genesis 2:18, NKJV)

This was not a contradiction. It was a revelation of purpose. Only God can remain One and be all-sufficient. *"The Lord our God, the Lord is one!"* (Deuteronomy 6:4) But for man to fulfill his assignment of multiplication, he had to be divided.

From Singularity to Family: The Pattern of Sonship

God alone is Jehovah, the self-existing One. He requires nothing outside Himself to be whole. He is singular, complete, and eternal. But when God made man, He did not duplicate His self-sufficiency; He extended His likeness into relational dependency. He made man to be a son, and sonship finds expression not in singularity but in family.

"God sets the solitary in families…" Psalm 68:6, NKJV

"Where two or three are gathered in My name, there I am in the midst of them." Matthew 18:20, NKJV

God's plan was never for man to exist in isolation or autonomous strength. True sonship is not realized in being alone, it's revealed in relationship: brethren, covenant, community, and unity. The household of faith is not a metaphor; it's a Kingdom reality. Sons are formed, affirmed, and matured in family, not in the wilderness of individualism.

God may be One, but He desires many sons (Hebrews 2:10). He may exist singularly, but He expresses Himself through plurality.

We are not self-existing; we are son-existing.

Our purpose is not realized in separation, but in connection.

God didn't form woman from the dust again, He split Adam to multiply Adam. What was originally one was now two, but still "all one" in divine purpose.

"So God created man in His own image; in the image of God He created him; male and female He created them." (Genesis 1:27, NKJV)

This division was not dysfunction, it was design. The splitting of man wasn't the breaking of unity but the birth of community, the seedbed of multiplication, and the unfolding of Kingdom order. The family was born, not of separate origin, but of shared essence.

Adam could not fulfill his assignment alone. Dominion required difference. Sons of the Kingdom would come from the womb of unity divided for multiplication.

The Likeness of God in the Woman

Some have, through a narrow hermeneutical lens, concluded that Eve was not made in God's image, since she was formed from Adam's rib rather than directly from the dust. But such a view overlooks the divine logic of Genesis 1:27, where male and female together reflect the image of God.

When God formed woman from man, He did not start over. He did not recreate the woman, He formed her, but from a different substance than man. He fashioned her out of Adam, because what was in Adam was already complete in essence. The difference was her form not her essence.

"So the Lord God caused a deep sleep to fall on Adam… and He took one of his ribs… Then the rib which the Lord God

19

had taken from man He made into a woman." (Genesis 2:21–22, NKJV)

Formed Individually, Created Simultaneously

It is essential to understand that while God created male and female simultaneously, He formed them individually. Genesis 1:27 reveals the moment of divine intention:

"So God created man in His own image; in the image of God He created him; male and female He created them." (NKJV)

This was the creation of mankind, male and female together, within the eternal counsel and image of God. But in Genesis 2, we are shown how that divine intention was formed into reality. Adam was formed first from the dust, and Eve was formed second from his side, not as an afterthought, but as a deliberate expression of distinction and unity.

God did not create Eve independently from Adam; He formed her independently. Her origin was not separate from Adam's essence, because their creation was singular in spirit but dual in form.

The Hebrew word 'adam in Genesis 1:27–28 refers to humanity, mankind, not merely to one male individual.

This is critical in the conversation of sonship. In the Kingdom, sonship is not gendered, it is positional. Both male and female were created in the image of God. Both were blessed. Both were given dominion. And both were included in the command to "be fruitful and multiply." Thus, both share in the original calling of sonship, even as they walk in distinct functions.

Eve was not an accessory to Adam's identity. She was a participant in the same calling: to walk in likeness, image, and dominion as a son of God.

Adam was formed from the dust of the ground; Eve was built from Adam's side. Their forms were different, but their essence was the same. She did not need to be formed from the earth again, because what was in Adam already carried the image and likeness of God.

*"This is the book of the genealogy of Adam. In the day that God created man (adam), He made him in the likeness of God. He created them male and female, and blessed them and **called them Mankind (adam)** in the day they were created."* (Genesis 5:1–2, NKJV)

The Hebrew word **'adam** is used for both the man and for mankind collectively.

Genesis 5:2 says *"He called their name Adam"* (KJV), or *"He called them Mankind"* (NKJV, NIV), which indicates that male and female shared the same name; adam, from the beginning.

This shows that the image-bearing identity was mutual, and the name Adam (which also means "man" or "human") was not exclusive to the male but applied to both male and female as one humanity.

"Male and female He created them..." (Genesis 1:27, NKJV)

When God took from Adam to make the woman, He was not giving her a secondhand identity, He was giving her a distinct formation. The difference was not in value or image, but in form and function. She was not created as a lesser being, but as a complementary expression of the same divine image.

To say that Eve was not made in the image of God because she came from Adam is to misunderstand the nature of image-bearing. Adam's image came from God; Eve's came through Adam from God. It was not diminished in the transfer, it was multiplied through distinction.

This means the likeness of God that had been imparted to Adam was also in the woman, because she came from the man who had received God's image and likeness.

She was not less divine, less authoritative, or less like God. She was the continuation of image-bearing, expressed in feminine distinction.

The woman did not carry a separate revelation, she carried a shared essence. Together, male and female represented the full relational capacity of God's image in creation.

Together, They Made Up Sonship

The woman did not carry a separate revelation; she carried a shared essence. Together, male and female represented the full relational capacity of God's image in creation. God did not reveal Himself as Father through the man alone, but through the oneness of two, distinct in form, united in essence.

This was not the creation of two separate beings, but of one shared sonship expressed through two distinct forms. Sonship, from the beginning, was not about gender, it was about bearing God's image in covenant relationship. Together, they formed the foundation of Kingdom sonship on earth. Together, they reflected the relational glory of the Godhead.

Together, they were called Adam, not because they were the same, but because they were one. And in that oneness, they revealed the fullness of God's intent: sons in His image, multiplied through unity.

God's image was never meant to be monopolized by one gender but multiplied through unity.

One Name, Two Distinctions: Clarifying Biblical Unity

Genesis 5:2 reveals a powerful truth:

"He created them male and female, and blessed them and called them 'Mankind' in the day they were created." (Genesis 5:2, NKJV)

This verse confirms that God gave both male and female a shared identity as adam (mankind). But this unity of name does not mean a blurring of distinction. On the contrary, it affirms that while both man and woman bear the image and likeness of God, they do so through divinely ordained differences. God is not the author of confusion (1 Corinthians 14:33). He created male and female, two distinct, complementary expressions of His likeness, both capable of reflecting His glory, yet not interchangeable.

This truth does not support any idea of gender fluidity or modern reinterpretations of identity. Rather, it reveals that God's original design for image-bearing sonship includes both men and women in functional distinction and spiritual unity.

Sonship: Oneness in Distinction

Ultimately, the creation narrative of mankind reveals a foundational truth: sonship is portrayed in oneness made up of difference. God did not create isolated beings to reflect His image; He formed a union. He divided the one into two, not to divide, but to multiply and to reveal that relational unity is central to sonship.

Sonship cannot exist in isolation. It is non-existent outside of plurality in unity, and multiplicity in singleness. This divine paradox, two becoming one, echoes the very nature of God Himself: Father, Son, and Spirit, distinct in person, one in essence.

Likewise, Adam and Eve bore the image of the Godhead, not independently, but interdependently. Their unity was not sameness; it was covenantal oneness. And in that oneness, the image of God was seen, the authority of dominion was shared, and the assignment to multiply was activated.

In Kingdom terms, sonship is not a solo identity, it is a family identity. It is the many in the One. The sons of God are not formed in isolation, but in communion, community, and covenant.

Mankind as Sons: The Inclusive Nature of Sonship

If Luke's Gospel is accurate, and we know it is, then Adam was not just the first man, but the first son of God (Luke 3:38, NKJV). This means that mankind itself, both male and female, is viewed through the lens of sonship. Genesis 1:27 affirms that male and female were created together, even though they were later formed individually. They were two distinct persons, yet one shared essence, one divine image.

"He created them male and female and blessed them and called them Mankind in the day they were created." (Genesis 5:2, NKJV)

In Hebrew thought, to say "Adam" or "man" often meant humanity, not just the male. So, when both male and female are present, it is appropriate to say mankind is present. Likewise, when both male and female believers are gathered, it is biblically appropriate to say the sons of God are present, because sonship in the Kingdom is not gendered, but positional.

"But as many as received him, to them gave he power to become the sons of God, even to them that believe on his name:" (John 1:12, KJV)

Though some translations say "children," the original Greek word huios used throughout the New Testament signifies sons, a legal term conveying inheritance, identity, and status. It is not exclusionary to men or women; rather, it is inclusive of all who are born of God, giving both male and female full status as heirs.

Paul reinforces this truth:

"There is neither male nor female; for you are all one in Christ Jesus. And if you are Christ's, then you are Abraham's seed, and heirs according to the promise." (Galatians 3:28–29, NKJV)

In the Kingdom, sonship is not about gender, it's about inheritance. Both men and women are adopted into the family of God through Christ and given the full rights of sons.

"Be fruitful and multiply…" wasn't a command to fill the earth with random people. It was a command to fill the earth with sons of God, those who walk in His image, likeness, and dominion.

Adam, mankind, was the first son. Not merely a man, but a bearer of God's image and likeness. He was built, not born, yet breathed into by the Father Himself

Through the fall, identity was not cancelled. The Father still called him by name, sonship remained the blueprint.

As we journey through the chapters ahead, we will trace the story of sonship from the garden to the cross, from broken identity to restored inheritance. We will uncover the orphan spirit that clouds our view, rediscover the adoption that makes us heirs, and awaken to the truth that we were never called to be slaves, but sons of God.

The Kingdom begins with sonship, and so must we.

REFLECTION QUESTIONS

1. How does viewing Adam as the first son of God, not just the first man, reshape your understanding of your own origin and purpose?

_____

_____

_____

_____

2. In what ways have you misunderstood identity by focusing on behavior (good vs. evil) rather than image and likeness?

_____

_____

_____

_____

_____

3. How does the concept of "plurality in unity" challenge or strengthen your understanding of what it means to walk in sonship today?

_____

_____

_____

_____

_____

4. Can you identify areas where your personal perception has shaped your reality more than God's truth, like Adam or the prodigal son?

_____

_____

_____

_____

_____

_____

5. What would it look like for you to live in fellowship with the Father, rather than striving to earn what He already gave in sonship?

_____

_____

_____

_____

_____

_____

_____

_____

_____

_____

_____

_____

NOTES

_____

_____

_____

_____

_____

_____

_____

_____

_____

_____

_____

_____

_____

_____

_____

_____

_____

_____

_____

_____

_____

_____

"At the heart of
the ministry of the Spirit
is sonship."
— Jack Miller

CHAPTER 2
THE ORPHAN SPIRIT

I have a confession to make.

For years, when I heard the phrase "orphan spirit," I dismissed it as little more than a spiritual cliché, a trendy term thrown around in inner healing circles to label people's emotional wounds or unresolved trauma. It sounded like psychology wrapped in religious language. To me, it lacked theological depth and felt too subjective to be meaningful.

But I've come to realize it is far more than an emotional descriptor. It is the condition of fallen humanity. It's not just a feeling of abandonment, it is a spiritual posture birthed in the garden and inherited by all mankind until Christ came to restore us.

For much of my life in ministry, I thought I was operating from sonship because I understood the language. I taught it. I affirmed others in it. But inwardly, I often labored under pressure, comparison, and striving, subtle signals that I was still trying to earn what I already had. I called God "Father," but I lived like an orphan, always doing, never resting.

The moment I realized I had spent years working for approval that was already mine was the moment everything changed. The Father didn't rebuke me, He embraced me. He wasn't waiting for me to perform; He was waiting for me to return. And what I've come to know is this: the orphan spirit is not some fringe dysfunction; it is the silent default mode of every heart that hasn't been fully convinced of the Father's love.

But looking back, I now realize something even deeper. I lived with what I would call sovereign responsibility, a weight I was never meant to carry. If there was a need, I rushed to meet it. If someone was hurting, I assumed it was mine to fix. If someone lacked, I believed it was my job to provide. I didn't pray first, I planned. I didn't run to the Father, I said, "I'll take care of it." It sounds noble, but it was actually orphan thinking dressed up as responsibility.

"The orphan spirit causes you to live like a spiritual orphan, independent, self-reliant, driven to succeed, and focused on what you can do instead of who you are." Jack Frost

My instinct was always, "How can I help?" or "What can I do?", and while that sounds compassionate, it subtly exposed a deeper belief: that I was alone, that the burden was mine, and that help wasn't coming unless I became the help. I never doubted God's love for others, but I wasn't convinced He would show up for me. So, I overcompensated. I tried to be everything for everyone, believing that's what sons do.

But sons don't live like gods. Sons trust the Father.

It's taken time, and still takes intentional surrender, to stop leading with "I've got this" and start learning to say, "Father, what are You doing here?" I'm learning that being present doesn't mean being the answer. Sometimes it means simply pointing to the Father who always was.

Sonship isn't something I discovered in a sermon or grasped in a moment, it's something I am still growing into daily.

And that's the invitation of this chapter: to awaken to what you already are. A son.

Another layer of my orphan mindset was how I related to God in prayer, particularly when it came to asking for things for myself. For years, I avoided it. And to this day, I still wrestle with it. Somewhere along the way, rooted in childhood disappointments and unmet expectations, I stopped asking.

I had believed for things before. Hoped. Waited. Trusted. And it didn't turn out the way I thought it would. So instead of continuing in relational trust, I defaulted to a kind of theological logic: "God is omniscient, He knows what I need. He's Omnipotent, He can do whatever He wants. So, if I don't have it, He must not want me to."

It sounded spiritual. But it wasn't trust, it was resignation. I abandoned the relational component of petition. I wasn't coming as a son who asks and settled into a cold kind of sovereignty: "Whatever will be, will be." My prayers were no longer conversations with a Father. They became executive briefings with a divine CEO.

I had a great working relationship with God. I was obedient, called, and committed to the mission. But intimacy was absent. Petition was uncomfortable. Sonship was virtually non-existent. I didn't know how to receive because I didn't know how to ask. And I didn't ask because I didn't really believe I was supposed to, not as a son, anyway.

But sons ask. Sons come boldly. Sons don't beg, but they do believe their Father delights in blessing them, not just using them. I'm learning that again. Slowly. Painfully. Beautifully.

"The orphan spirit is not about being without parents, it's about feeling disconnected from your Source, your Father, and your identity." Dr. Mark Chironna

It is not merely emotional, it is existential. The orphan spirit is what entered the heart of man when he transgressed, when fear replaced trust, and when performance replaced identity.

How the Fall Created the Orphan Mindset

When Adam sinned, the first thing that entered wasn't guilt, it was fear.

Not fear of punishment, but fear rooted in perceived disconnection.

"I heard Your voice in the garden, and I was afraid because I was naked; and I hid myself." (Genesis 3:10, NKJV)

The orphan mindset was born the moment Adam said, "I was afraid... and I hid." Fear became the lens, and hiding became the habit. From that moment on, humanity began building lives of performance, walls of self-protection, and a theology of distance from a Father who never moved.

Like Adam, my fear didn't come from God, it came from a distorted perception of self. Adam hid not because he stopped being a son, but because he stopped believing he was one.

I found myself wrestling with the same fear, not as a fleeting emotion, but as a spiritual adversary. I contended with it, rebuked it, fought it like an enemy of faith. But over time, I realized it wasn't merely the presence of fear that had gripped me. It was the absence of the Father's love. I didn't recognize it then. I wasn't prepared to receive love, especially not the kind a Father gives to a son.

Deep down, I expected love to come with strings attached. I believed I would somehow owe God for loving me, that it wasn't truly free. My idea of love had been shaped by human failure, conditional, fractured, inconsistent. If people couldn't love me unconditionally, how could I believe God did? My standard for love had been corrupted, and so I struggled to receive what the Father offered. What I needed was not a better performance, but a better standard. I didn't need to work harder. I needed the Father. But He was waiting for me to stop striving and simply be a son.

Like the prodigal, I often lived in the mindset of a servant. "I've failed. I've wasted so much. I'm not worthy to be called a son. Just let me serve." That's how I felt, and how I approached God: committed, loyal, but distant. But the Father wasn't waiting with a contract. He was holding out a robe. A ring. Shoes for my feet. He didn't want my penance. He wanted me, fully restored. He never stopped calling me son. I was the one who struggled to believe it.

The tree of the knowledge of good and evil didn't just bring death; it brought judgment, a new way of seeing oneself and others through the lens of moral performance. Instead of resting in likeness, man began striving for approval.

"Then the Lord God called to Adam and said to him, 'Where are you?'" (Genesis 3:9, NKJV)

God never called him "sinner." He didn't rename him "failure." He called him by the name of sonship, Adam, because relationship had not been revoked, Adam only believed it had.

The most important thing I had to learn, and what every believer must come to understand, is this: behavior doesn't change identity. The fall didn't cancel Adam's sonship; it confused it. Sin warped his perception, not God's position. The knowledge of good and evil, right and wrong, became a flawed measuring stick in the limited mind of humanity. From that point forward, mankind began labeling themselves by behavior rather than by design. But correction was never meant to rebrand identity. God never called Adam a sinner. He never revoked his name. He asked, "Where are you?", a question rooted in relationship, not rejection. Behavior may require correction, but identity must be preserved. The Father does not disown sons who stumble. He restores them.

This is where so many of us miss it. We've confused correction with condemnation, and discipline with disqualification. Instead of running to the Father, we run from Him, ashamed, uncertain, and unwilling to believe that love can be unconditional. We begin to live by effort instead of by essence. Like the prodigal rehearsing a servant's speech, we come back home hoping for tolerance instead of restoration. But the Father doesn't just want us back in the house, He wants us back in the family. And until we receive that truth, we'll keep wearing the clothes of a servant in a house built for sons.

Many believers call God 'Father' but live like orphans. They serve in the house but never feel at home. They strive for approval, fear rejection, and view God more like a judge than a Father.

Yet from the beginning, God created sons, image-bearers, formed not just to function, but to fellowship.

"I will not leave you orphans; I will come to you." – John 14:18 (NKJV)

If the disciples (and, by extension, all humanity) were never in danger of feeling or functioning as orphans, this assurance would make little sense. Jesus is acknowledging two realities at once:

Firstly, an experiential orphanhood. They already sensed impending abandonment *("Where are You going?"* v. 5). Since Eden, fear and self-reliance had taught mankind, *"We're on our own."*

Secondly, Jesus affirms ontological sonship, which means that being a son is part of your very nature and design. It's not something you earn or qualify for through performance; it is who you are because of how God created you. When Jesus says, "I will not leave you as orphans," He isn't calling them orphans in their identity, but acknowledging how they feel, disconnected, alone, unsure of their place.

His words suggest that they belong to a family but have forgotten or doubted that truth. Their sonship hasn't been revoked, it has been obscured by fear, shame, and disconnection. Jesus' statement is a loving reminder that He is not creating sons out of strangers, He is restoring sons who had forgotten the Father's embrace.

So, John 14:18 confirms the orphan spirit is both a condition we live under and a perception we believe. Christ's remedy is not simply to comfort emotions but to restore the confidence that sin, and the fear it spawned, stole. The Spirit He sends (v. 16-17) is the living guarantee that we are not fatherless; we never were.

Jesus didn't just come to die for sin, He came to restore sonship.

What exactly is an "Orphan Spirit"?

The orphan spirit is not a demon, it is a mindset. It is the inner sense of abandonment, striving, and spiritual homelessness birthed from the fall, where Adam and Eve lost their awareness of God's presence and likeness.

Symptoms of the orphan mentality include, striving for approval instead of resting in love, fear of rejection instead of trusting God's acceptance, hyper-independence and self-reliance, comparison and jealousy and insecurity and rejection

There are practical steps to address these symptoms.

Striving for Approval

Identifying characteristics: Constant performance, people-pleasing, burnout

A root cause is belief that love must be earned

Kingdom Cure:

Rest in God's unconditional love: "This is My beloved Son, in whom I am well pleased" (Matthew 3:17)

Identity before activity means you are not loved because of what you do; you are loved for who you are.

Fear of Rejection or Abandonment

Identifying characteristics are isolation, anxiety, needing to be needed.

A root cause is the belief that God or people will leave or abandon you.

Kingdom Cure:

The answers to the fear of rejection or abandonment are found in scripture. Romans 8:38–39 says *"Nothing can separate us from the love of God"*. Further affirmed: You are accepted in the Beloved (Ephesians 1:6)

Community healing: Orphans isolate; sons trust safe relationships and grow in family.

"The servant is accepted because of his obedience. The son is obedient because he is accepted."

— Richard Foster

Independence and Control

Identifying characteristics: Refusal to ask for help, needing to be in charge

A root cause is belief that no one is trustworthy or capable

Kingdom Cure:

John 5:19 — Jesus only did what He saw the Father doing Dependency on God is maturity, not weakness

Invite Holy Spirit into your daily decisions: surrender and trust replaces control

Comparison and Jealousy

Identifying characteristics: Insecurity around others' success, hidden competition

A root cause is belief that love, and resources are scarce

Kingdom Cure:

Luke 15:31 — "All that I have is yours" Celebrate others intentionally, joyfully sow honor. Understand that in the Kingdom, there is no scarcity, each son has an inheritance.

Insecurity and Self-Rejection

Identifying characteristics: Low self-worth, shame, needing validation

A root cause is belief that you are flawed and unworthy of love

Kingdom Cure:

1 John 3:1 — *"Behold what manner of love the Father has given us, that we should be called children of God!"* Replace lies with identity declarations (Romans 8, Ephesians 1–2)

Begin to speak sonship truths over yourself

Walk in gratitude, thankfulness shifts scarcity into abundance

Jesus: The Model of Sonship

Jesus is the perfect picture of sonship. From baptism to the wilderness, to the cross, Jesus never operated from striving, but from the certainty of being the Beloved Son.

"This is My beloved Son, in whom I am well pleased." – Matthew 3:17 (NKJV)

This was spoken before He performed any miracles, or officially entered His earthly ministry. Identity preceded activity. Jesus never forgot nor forsook these words.

At His temptation, satan tried to provoke Jesus to prove Himself, *"If You are the Son of God…"*. But Jesus never took the bait. Sons don't perform for identity; they live from it.

"The enemy's goal isn't just to tempt you, it's to get you to forget who you are." Graham Cooke

The Devil Went After His Sonship, Not His Susceptibility

When Jesus was tempted in the wilderness, the enemy didn't attack His desires, He attacked His designation.

He didn't go after His susceptibility, because Jesus had none. He went after His sonship, because that's where authority, identity, and inheritance reside.

The enemy's strategy hasn't changed since Eden:

41

In the garden, satan twisted the truth of what God said to Adam and Eve.

In the wilderness, he twisted the truth of what God said about Jesus.

"This is My beloved Son, in whom I am well pleased." – Matthew 3:17 (NKJV)

...was immediately followed by,

"If You are the Son of God..."

This proves that temptation isn't merely about behavior, it's about identity.

Temptation is not a test of how weak you are.

It's a test of how secure you are in your identity as a son.

When we talk about the orphan spirit, we're not just referring to emotional dysfunction or fatherlessness, we're talking about an identity war. The orphan spirit is a counterfeit mindset that says you are separate, unwanted, and unworthy of love, inheritance, and belonging. It whispers:

"You have to prove yourself to be accepted."

"You're alone—no one is coming for you."

"You must survive on your own."

But Jesus, the true and faithful Son, never yielded to that voice, not even once.

The Wilderness Was a Battle Over Sonship

Jesus had no sin. He wasn't drawn away by lust or fear. The temptation was not to sin morally but to act independently, to step outside of trust and relationship with the Father.

That's the core of the orphan spirit: It tempts sons to act like they're alone. But Jesus never surrendered. He didn't perform, panic, or prove anything. He stood in the confidence of the Father's affirmation.

Sons Don't Prove. They Abide.

When satan said, *"Turn these stones into bread,"*

Jesus didn't answer with effort, He answered with truth.

"It is written, 'Man shall not live by bread alone, but by every word that proceeds from the mouth of God." (Matthew 4:4, NKJV)

He lived from what the Father had already spoken.

He trusted in His identity as Son, even in hunger, isolation, and spiritual attack. He refused the orphan's lie: *"You're on your own."*

What we learn from Jesus: He didn't question the Father's love in the silence. He didn't trade identity for survival. He didn't respond to accusation with performance.

Even in nakedness, suffering, and death, He never lost the revelation of Sonship.

In His final moments on the cross, when darkness covered the land and He bore the crushing weight of humanity's sin, Jesus made a profound declaration:

"Father, into Your hands I commit My spirit." (Luke 23:46, NKJV)

He did not echo the words of the prodigal son,

"I am no longer worthy to be called your son" (Luke 15:19).

Instead, He called Him Father.

Even while **becoming** sin (2 Corinthians 5:21) and experiencing the anguish of physical torture, Jesus never questioned His identity. He didn't crumble under the lie of unworthiness. He committed Himself into the loving hands of His Father, not as a criminal or a slave, but as a Son.

This Was the Final Blow to the Orphan Spirit

Jesus didn't resist the orphan mindset by rebuking it. He resisted it by refusing to become it. He died without shame, even while bearing ours. His last breath was not despair, it was faith in the Father's love.

The greatest weapon against the orphan spirit is unwavering trust in sonship.

Jesus never lost that trust, not in the wilderness, not in the Garden, and not on the cross. Jesus defeated the orphan spirit not by rebuking it, but by never becoming it.

He showed us that true warfare is not about casting out devils, it's about standing firm in who you are. When you know you are a son, the orphan spirit loses all power.

If you've ever been tempted to prove, perform, or compromise, remember, the enemy is after your identity, not your ability. He wants you to doubt your "belovedness", not just fail in your behavior. Sons don't strive to become sons; they live from the assurance that they already are.

Jesus overcame the orphan spirit in the wilderness by refusing to argue, prove, or perform. He stood in what the Father had already spoken.

Contrast Chart:

Orphan	Son
Seeks validation	Lives from affirmation
Fears lack	Trusts the Father's provision
Competes for place	Knows they belong
Performs for love	Rests in love
Leads to burnout	Leads to overflow

Renewing Your Mind

Transformation begins in the mind. You must uproot orphan thinking and replace it with truth.

"Do not be conformed to this world but be transformed by the renewing of your mind..." – Romans 12:2 (NKJV)

John 8:35 – You are a son, not a servant.
Galatians 4:7 – You are no longer a slave, but a son.
Ephesians 1:5-6 – You are accepted in the Beloved

"Many of us live with a deep inner sense of being an unworthy, unloved child. This is the great lie." Henri Nouwen

The orphan spirit is not just an emotional wound, it is a spiritual deception. It is the lie that says you're alone, unloved, and must earn what only a Father can give freely. But Jesus shattered that lie. He never surrendered to it.

He never whispered, *"I'm unworthy."*

Even while hanging in naked shame, He called God *"Father."*

And because of Him, so can you. You were not made to wander through life trying to prove your worth. You were never meant to survive on scraps, fear, or self-preservation. You were born for a table, a robe, a ring, and a Father's embrace.

The orphan spirit dies where sonship is received. You are not disqualified. You are not forgotten. You are not alone. In Christ, you are a son. So silence the voice that tells you to strive, to fear, to hide.

Overcoming an orphan mentality requires a shift in identity, moving from a mindset of lack, fear, and striving to one of sonship, trust, and inheritance in the Father.

Overcoming an orphan mentality is not a matter of behavior modification, it is a deep shift of identity.

It's the journey of moving from a mindset of lack, fear, and striving into the reality of sonship, trust, and inheritance in the Father. The orphan heart operates from a place of survival; the son walks in confidence and rest, knowing he belongs.

Before healing can begin, the orphan mindset must first be recognized. It's not always dramatic or obvious. It often hides behind responsibility, independence, or even spiritual performance. It shows up in subtle ways: striving for approval instead of resting in love, fearing lack rather than trusting in God's provision, or functioning from self-reliance rather than dependency on the Father.

Orphans compare and compete; sons celebrate others. Orphans feel rejected and unwanted; sons walk in the confidence of being chosen.

The transformation begins with renewing the mind. Romans 12:2 exhorts us not to be conformed to the world's patterns but to be transformed by the renewing of our minds.

This isn't just about positive thinking, it's about receiving the truth of who you are in Christ. You are not a servant trying to earn a place. You are a son who belongs in the Father's house (John 8:35; Galatians 4:7). You are fully accepted in the

Beloved (Ephesians 1:5–6). You are an heir, not a beggar, with full access to the Kingdom (Romans 8:17).

But renewing the mind isn't enough if we still relate to God as a distant figure rather than a loving Father. Jesus came to reveal the Father, not just to forgive sin.

When He told His disciples, *"If you've seen Me, you've seen the Father,"* He was inviting them into a relational reality that changes everything (John 14:9–18).

Jesus' words in John 14:9, "He who has seen Me has seen the Father," hold a weight far deeper than mere representation. They speak of a oneness that is not symbolic but essential, a union that goes beyond mission or message and flows from the very nature of divine relationship. In this one phrase, Jesus dismantles every image of a distant, detached, or unknowable God. He is not saying, "I remind you of the Father." He is saying, "I am the visible expression of the Father you've longed to know."

This statement is the beating heart of sonship. It reveals that Jesus didn't just teach about the Father, He lived in seamless union with Him. His identity was not separate from His relationship. He never wrestled to earn approval. He never wondered if He belonged. He never questioned His value or place in the Father's heart. Everything He did, every healing, every word, every act of obedience, flowed from the settled confidence that He was the beloved Son.

Jesus said plainly, "I and the Father are one." This was not metaphor. It was ontological truth, a truth of being. To see Jesus is to see the Father. The fullness of the invisible God was made visible in the life and love of Christ. He didn't simply reflect the Father's will, He radiated the Father's heart.

This is why the orphan spirit is so dangerous. It operates in direct opposition to this kind of union. The orphan mindset lives from a sense of separation rather than connection. It strives instead of abides. It views God as distant or demanding rather than present and loving. Orphans constantly ask, "Am I enough?" or "What must I do to be accepted?" They live in the shadows of doubt and the constant pressure to prove their worth.

Jesus never lived this way. He didn't wonder if the Father loved Him; He rested in that love. He didn't perform to be accepted; He ministered from the security of His identity. This is the antidote to the orphan spirit, certainty in the Father's presence, confidence in His love, and unwavering trust in our place as sons.

When Jesus told Philip, "If you've seen Me, you've seen the Father," He was addressing more than just a theological curiosity. He was answering the ache of generations. Ever since the fall, mankind has wrestled with a distorted view of God. Fear replaced fellowship. Distance replaced intimacy. Performance replaced identity. But Jesus came to change all of that. He didn't come just to inform us of what the Father is like, He came to invite us into the relationship He shares with the Father.

This invitation is more than comfort, it's transformation. Jesus restores not only our view of God but our place with God. He doesn't just show us who the Father is. He shows us who we are in the Father's eyes. The statement, "If you've seen Me, you've seen the Father," becomes a mirror, not just of divinity, but of destiny. It is a call to walk in the same sonship He lived in, to abide in the same love, to stand in the same confidence.

Jesus did not speak this from a platform of privilege, but from a position of surrender. He lived in union with the Father, and He invites us into that same union. In that light, the orphan spirit becomes powerless. Its whispers of separation, striving, and shame fall silent in the presence of perfect love.

"What comes into our minds when we think about God is the most important thing about us." A.W. Tozer

This is the deepest truth of the gospel, not only that Jesus came to save us, but that He came to bring us home. If you've seen Him, you've seen the Father. And if you've received Him, you've received the Spirit of sonship. You are no longer a stranger or servant, you are a son, seated in the same love, carrying the same name.

"Therefore you are no longer a slave but a son, and if a son, then an heir of God through Christ." Galatians 4:7 (NKJV)

Jesus didn't die merely to change your status; He came to restore your relationship. When He said, "I no longer call you servants, I call you sons," He wasn't just offering a new label. He was declaring a new way of living, loving, and relating to God. Sons don't just obey orders, they receive inheritance, walk in access, and dwell in the presence of their Father.

But even this revelation would remain incomplete without the work of the Holy Spirit.

The Holy Spirit is not just a power to perform signs and wonders. He is the Person who brings us into intimacy with the Father. While the law demanded obedience from a distance, the Spirit draws us into closeness through adoption. As Paul writes, "You did not receive the spirit of bondage again to fear, but you received the Spirit of adoption by whom we cry out, 'Abba, Father.'" (Romans 8:15, NKJV)

This cry of "Abba" isn't merely emotional, it's ontological. It arises from a reawakened identity. It's not something you muster up. It's something the Spirit stirs within you. When the Holy Spirit enters your life, He doesn't teach you how to perform for God; He testifies that you already belong to God.

Verse 16 continues, *"The Spirit Himself bears witness with our spirit that we are children of God."*

This is more than comfort, it's confirmation. The Spirit comes as witness, not to our performance, but to our position. He testifies to the truth of sonship even when your emotions contradict it, even when fear whispers otherwise. He doesn't wait until you act like a son; He affirms that you are one.

The Spirit of adoption restores the sound that was lost in Eden, the sound of sons walking confidently with their Father in the cool of the day. That cry, "Abba," is the heartbeat of restored relationship. It is the voice of sonship echoing again through creation, silencing the orphan's lie and welcoming us home. Prayer becomes relational. God is no longer a distant deity but a present Father.

This changes how we approach love. Orphans feel they must perform for love. Sons receive love freely and securely. When we meditate on the love the Father has lavished upon us (1 John 3:1), our identity begins to solidify. We no longer work to be seen or strive to be enough. We realize we are already loved.

And from that love comes access. Orphans live in spiritual survival mode, always waiting for the next blow or fearing that their provision will run out. Sons, however, walk in peace. They understand that everything the Father has is already theirs. They don't beg for scraps. They live seated with Christ in heavenly places (Ephesians 2:6), ruling with Him, not trying to earn proximity.

For many, the orphan mentality is rooted in deep father wounds, painful experiences, neglect, or the absence of affirmation. Earthly fathers, no matter how present, cannot fill the eternal ache meant to be satisfied only by our heavenly Father.

Healing comes when we allow God to redefine fatherhood and heal the places broken by human failure. As Psalm 68:5 declares, He is *"a Father to the fatherless."* He fills the gaps no one else can.

And sonship isn't just personal, it's communal. Orphans isolate, protect, and compete. But sons know they are part of a family. They live connected, not just to God, but to His body. According to Ephesians 2:19, we are no longer strangers but members of the household of God. Healing often accelerates in community, not in isolation. The Church is not meant to be a company of performers, but a family of sons and daughters walking in covenant love.

Finally, the posture of a son is gratitude and rest. Where the orphan fears loss, the son knows his Father owns everything. The Father told the older brother in Luke 15:31, *"All that I have is yours."*

Gratitude shifts us from scarcity to abundance. We stop fearing what we don't have and begin stewarding what we've already been given. From that place, we walk in peace.

To overcome the orphan mentality is to say yes to sonship. It is not a one-time revelation but a daily return to the Father's love, a continual resting in His embrace, and a growing maturity in the truth: you are no longer a slave, but a son.

Step out of the shadows and into the Father's house. The door has never been closed. Because you've never been unwanted, only unawakened. And today, you awaken.

Endnotes & References

Jack Frost, From Spiritual Slavery to Spiritual Sonship, Shiloh Place Ministries, 2006.

Leif Hetland, Healing the Orphan Spirit, Destiny Image Publishers, 2011.

Bill Johnson, Hosting the Presence: Unveiling Heaven's Agenda, Destiny Image Publishers, 2012.

Key Biblical Foundations: Romans 8:15–16; Galatians 4:6–7; John 14:18; Ephesians 1:5–6; Matthew 3:17; Luke 23:46.

Note: The term "orphan spirit" does not appear verbatim in Scripture but reflects a theological interpretation developed by several authors and teachers to describe the mindset of disconnection from God as Father.

Reflection Questions

1. When you hear the phrase "orphan spirit," what thoughts or assumptions come to mind? Have they changed after reading this chapter?

_____

_____

_____

_____

2. Can you identify a time in your life when fear, performance, or hiding became your default response to God?

_____

_____

_____

_____

_____

3. Which symptoms of the orphan mindset (e.g., striving, comparison, fear of rejection) do you most recognize in your own life?

_____

_____

_____

_____

_____

4. Jesus never surrendered to the orphan mindset, even in His darkest hour. How does His example empower you to live in sonship today?

_____

_____

_____

_____

5. In what ways do you still try to earn what the Father gives freely?

_____

_____

_____

6. What does it look like for you to trust that "all the Father has is yours" (Luke 15:31)?

_____

_____

_____

7. How does Romans 8:15–16 (the Spirit crying 'Abba, Father') challenge or affirm how you approach God?

_____

_____

_____

_____

NOTES

_____

_____

_____

_____

_____

_____

_____

_____

_____

_____

_____

_____

_____

_____

_____

_____

_____

_____

_____

_____

CHAPTER 3
ABBA FATHER

"If you want to judge how well a person understands Christianity, find out how much they make of the thought of being God's child, and having God as their Father... For everything that Christ taught, everything that makes the New Testament new and better than the old, is summed up in the knowledge of the Fatherhood of God. 'Abba Father' is the Christian name for God." J.I. Packer ('Knowing God')

Most of Israel knew God as "El Shaddai" or "Yahweh," the Almighty, the Self-Existent One. But when Jesus walked among them, He didn't address God with formality. He shattered expectations by repeatedly calling Him "Father."

In fact, over 150 times in the Gospels, Jesus uses the word "Father", a term of intimacy that was foreign to many of His hearers.

This was not merely a stylistic choice. It was a divine revelation. Jesus didn't come simply to bring us to heaven; He came to bring us to the Father (John 14:6). He came not to start a religion, but to restore a relationship. And the doorway to that relationship is sonship.

Abba is not a title, it's a cry

"The word 'Abba', a term of intimacy and endearment, is the cry of a child who knows they are loved. To call God 'Abba' is to trust that you are embraced, even in your most broken state." Henri Nouwen

"Abba" is not the formal "Father," but the intimate plea of a child: "Papa." It's the Spirit's cry that confirms we are not just legally adopted but emotionally embraced. The Apostle Paul writes:

"For you did not receive the spirit of bondage again to fear, but you received the Spirit of adoption by whom we cry out, 'Abba, Father.' The Spirit Himself bears witness with our spirit that we are children of God."— Romans 8:15–16 (NKJV)

The Spirit of Adoption

Paul draws a contrast between two opposing spiritual states. Bondage to fear, the orphan mindset, rooted in law, shame, and insecurity, and adoption through the Spirit, the confident embrace of a Father who loves us.

Under the law, fear dominated. Under grace, love invites. The Spirit we've received is not one of distance but of belonging.

What "Adoption" Really Means

The Greek word for adoption is huiothesia—the placing of a son. In Roman culture, this wasn't second-class status. Adopted sons often had stronger legal standing than natural ones. They were chosen, named, and granted full inheritance.

Likewise, God has not merely forgiven us, He has named us. He has placed us as sons, not servants.

And this placement is sealed by the presence of His Spirit.

The dual cry: "Abba, Father"

Paul does something remarkable: he preserves the Aramaic word **"Abba"** and pairs it with the Greek word **"Pater."** This pairing speaks volumes. "Abba" conveys emotional intimacy. "Pater" speaks to legal authority and covenant inheritance.

When we cry "Abba, Father," we are not just appealing for help, we are echoing the cry of Jesus Himself (Mark 14:36). We are stepping into the same relationship Jesus had with the Father.

Kingdom Revelation: What This Cry Reveals

You are not an orphan needing permission to approach. You are not a servant hoping for attention. You are a son, both deeply loved and officially appointed.

This dual reality, intimacy and authority, is the heartbeat of Kingdom sonship.

The Spirit's cry within

Paul writes again in Galatians:

"And because you are sons, God has sent forth the Spirit of His Son into your hearts, crying out, 'Abba, Father!'" — Galatians 4:6 (NKJV)

This is not a phrase to memorize; it is a voice within. The Spirit's presence in you doesn't begin your sonship, it confirms it. You don't cry "Abba" to become a son. You cry "Abba" because you already are one.

What "Abba" and "Pater" Mean: Abba (Aramaic): Closeness, dependence, affection. A term used by toddlers. Pater (Greek): Lineage, inheritance, legal placement.

Together, these terms express the full spectrum of your relationship with God: the warmth of a child in his Father's arms, and the weight of an heir in his Father's house.

From knowledge to experience

Sonship is not merely doctrinal, it is deeply experiential. It affects how you pray, how you live, how you think.

Servant Prayers vs. Sonship Prayers

Orphan Prayers

"Please don't be angry…"
"I hope You hear me…"
"I hope You love me…"

Sonship Prayers

"Thank You for Your grace…"
"I know You hear me…"
"I know You love me…"

"Father, I thank You that You have heard Me. And I know that You always hear Me, but because of the people who are standing by I said this, that they may believe that You sent Me." John 11:41–42 (NKJV)

The Father's love

"The Father Himself loves you…" — John 16:27

The love of the Father is not performance-based. It is identity-based. He doesn't just love "the world", He loves you. Personally. Lavishly.

"Behold what manner of love the Father has bestowed on us, that we should be called children of God!" — 1 John 3:1

Trust is the evidence of sonship

Jesus trusted the Father in the Garden of Gethsemane, crying:

"Abba, Father… not My will, but Yours…" (Mark 14:36)

Sonship is revealed most, not in shouting declarations, but in quiet surrender. Obedience flows not from fear, but from trust.

Abiding in presence, not performance

"He made known His ways to Moses, His acts to the children of Israel." — Psalm 103:7

The children saw what God did. Moses knew why He did it.

Sons don't just want miracles, they want the Father. We grow not by effort, but by abiding (John 15:5). Presence matures us, relationship transforms us.

Eternal life is relational

"This is eternal life, that they may know You…"
— John 17:3

Knowing about God will never compare to knowing Him as Father. This is the great gift of Jesus, He brought us close.

He didn't just save us from sin; He introduced us to the Father.

Sonship is your birthright in Christ. The Spirit cries "Abba" not just in heaven, but in you. You are not distant, you are known, loved, and embraced.

The God Jesus revealed is not unreachable. He is Father. And in Christ, you are no longer a servant, but a son.

Reflection Questions

1. How has your understanding of God shifted from Judge or Master to Father?

_____

_____

_____

2. In what ways do you still pray like a servant rather than a son?

_____

_____

_____

3. Do you trust the Father when His will doesn't match your desires?

_____

_____

4. What does "Abba" mean to you personally?

_____

_____

5. How can you grow in relationship, not just responsibility, with the Father?

_____

_____

6. Am I relating to God from fear (as an orphan or servant) or from assurance (as a son)?

_____

_____

_____

_____

7. When I pray, is "Abba" my natural cry, or do I feel distant, unsure, and obligated to perform?

_____

_____

_____

8. Am I trying to gain what I already have? Or am I living from the cry of "Abba"?

_____

_____

_____

9. Do I only see God as "Father" in a formal sense, or do I truly experience Him as "Abba"?

_____

_____

_____

_____

NOTES

CHAPTER 4
Adopted into Glory

"For you did not receive the spirit of bondage again to fear, but you received the Spirit of adoption by whom we cry out, 'Abba, Father."
– Romans 8:15 (NKJV)

"...to bring many sons to glory..." – Hebrews 2:10 (NKJV)

Adoption: a divine legal transaction

Adoption is not a secondary status, it's a full placement with legal rights. The Greek word huiothesia means 'placing as a son.' This is not emotional; it's covenantal and permanent.

"...having predestined us to adoption as sons by Jesus Christ to Himself..." – Ephesians 1:5 (NKJV)

Adoption is not God's backup plan, it is His chosen way of revealing His glory through sons.

The Roman context: Paul's original meaning

Paul wrote to a Roman audience who understood adoption differently than Hebrews. In Roman culture:

Adopted sons had more privilege than biological ones, they were chosen. It was permanent and irrevocable. All debts and past associations were cancelled. The adoptee became a new person in the eyes of the law.

"Old things are passed away... all things become new." – 2
Corinthians 5:17 (NKJV)

From slavery to glory

"You did not receive the spirit of slavery again to fear..." –
Romans 8:15 (NKJV)

Paul's contrast is not between **sin** and **slavery** but **slavery**
and **sonship**. Many believers are freed from sin but still live
like slaves. Legalism replaces one form of bondage with
another. But adoption says: You belong.

This is not another kind of slavery. "Slavery again" reveals
we haven't been delivered from bondage to sin only to be
shackled again by religious performance or external
regulations. Sonship is not a new form of servitude with a
cleaner uniform. Paul is not saying we've swapped masters,
he's declaring that we've left slavery entirely.

"You did not receive the spirit of bondage again to fear,"
Paul writes, *"but you received the Spirit of adoption by
whom we cry out, 'Abba, Father'"* (Romans 8:15, NKJV).

This isn't God exchanging one set of chains for another. This
is the Father removing chains altogether and replacing them
with identity, inheritance, and intimacy.

We were never meant to serve God as slaves tiptoeing in
fear. We were made to walk with Him as sons secure in love.
God doesn't want our compliance based upon rules, He
wants our confidence based in love. He isn't demanding
submission from a distance, He's drawing us near through
the Spirit of adoption.

Sonship means we're not just free from sin, we're free from fear. We don't serve to earn a place at the table. We sit at the table because we belong. Sons are not motivated by obligation but by love. And that love casts out fear, especially the fear that we might not be enough.

This is not a call to stricter obedience. It's a call to deeper relationship. We are not simply pardoned prisoners, we are adopted children. Not hired hands in God's house, but heirs of His Kingdom.

"And if children, then heirs—heirs of God and joint heirs with Christ..." – Romans 8:17 (NKJV)

"It was fitting... to bring many sons to glory." – Hebrews 2:10 (NKJV)

The Spirit of adoption: how He testifies

The Holy Spirit's ministry is not just power, it's paternity. He cries out "Abba" through us, not in fear, but in love.

"The Spirit Himself bears witness with our spirit that we are children of God." – Romans 8:16 (NKJV)

Adopted into glory, not into bondage

Adoption is unto glory, honor, presence, dignity, and inheritance. Jesus is not ashamed to call us brothers (Hebrews 2:11). You were not adopted to serve at the gate but to sit at the table.

THE RIGHTS OF ADOPTION

As adopted sons, you have:
A new name – sealed in Christ
A new identity – no longer a slave
A new inheritance – joint-heirs with Christ
A permanent family – the household of God

"The gifts and the calling of God are irrevocable." –
Romans 11:29 (NKJV)

"I give them eternal life, and they shall never perish; neither shall anyone snatch them out of My hand." – John 10:28 (NKJV)

THE END GOAL IS SONSHIP INTO GLORY

"Those He foreknew, He also predestined to be conformed to the image of His Son..." – Romans 8:29 (NKJV)

God doesn't just want saved people, He wants glorified sons. Sonship is the vehicle; glory is the destination.

"For it was fitting for Him, for whom are all things and by whom are all things, in bringing many sons to glory, to make the captain of their salvation perfect through sufferings." Hebrews 2:10, NKJV

This verse contains the heart of sonship fulfilled, God's eternal plan to bring many sons to glory.

First, consider the phrase: *"It was fitting for Him…"*, the original Greek suggests it was morally appropriate, absolutely right, even beautiful in design that God would choose this path. The cross was not divine overreach or rescue improvisation. It was the glorious unveiling of God's predetermined plan: not just to save sinners, but to raise sons.

The goal was not merely forgiveness. The goal was glory. And not just Christ's glory, but shared glory. *"Bringing many sons to glory"* is not a sentimental phrase, it is a declaration of adoption, of elevation, of restored identity. Glory is not reserved for Christ alone; it is the intended inheritance of every son.

This glory is not fame, performance, or self-exaltation. It is the doxa of God, His intrinsic weight, worth, and reality, being revealed in and through sons. The same glory the first Adam lost is now restored in the Last Adam, who leads us out of the orphan wilderness and into the house of the Father.

"To make the captain of their salvation perfect through sufferings..."

Jesus did not lack perfection in His divinity. But in His humanity, He became our pioneer, our archēgos—the one who goes before. He blazed the trail of sonship not just by living sinlessly, but by suffering redemptively. His path to glory was marked by wounds, so ours could be marked by adoption.

He became like us, so we could become like Him.

And now He leads many, not a few, not just the deserving, but many sons to glory. Sons once covered in shame. Sons once convinced they were disqualified. Sons who had forgotten the sound of the Father's voice. Sons who had accepted the labels of slaves, servants, or survivors.

But now, through Him, we are brought, not just rescued, but brought, escorted into the glory we were always intended to carry. Not just saved from sin but crowned with the honor of sonship.

Hebrews 2:10 is more than a verse, it is a royal adoption decree. It declares that suffering was not the end, shame was not the final word, and death was not the inheritance. Glory is.

Because of Christ, you are not simply restored to Eden, you are raised to the right hand. You are not just forgiven, you are family. You are not just rescued, you are revealed. Sons brought to glory.

This is the language of inheritance, the posture of "belovedness", and the final blow to the orphan spirit.

Reflection Questions

1. What does Roman adoption reveal about how God sees you?

_____

_____

_____

2. In what areas of your life do you still live like a slave instead of a son?

_____

_____

_____

3. How has the Spirit of adoption ministered to you personally?

_____

_____

_____

4. What would change in your life if you truly believed your adoption was permanent?

_____

_____

_____

_____

CHRISTOPHER TURNEY

5. How can you live as one "adopted by glory" rather than one "rescued by guilt"?

_____

_____

_____

6. When you think of the phrase "bringing many sons to glory," do you see yourself included? Why or why not?

_____

_____

_____

_____

7. How does understanding that glory is your inheritance— not just Christ's reward—reshape your view of salvation?

_____

_____

_____

_____

8. Have you ever thought of your suffering as part of a journey toward sonship and glory? How might this change how you view your past or present challenges?

_____

_____

_____

_____

NOTES

CHAPTER 5
Discipline of sons

"For whom the Lord loves He chastens and scourges every son whom He receives." – Hebrews 12:6 (NKJV)

Discipline is the proof of sonship

Discipline is not rejection, it is confirmation. The presence of correction is not a sign that God is angry, but that you are a legitimate child.

"If you are without chastening... then you are illegitimate and not sons." – Hebrews 12:8 (NKJV)

Correction reveals identity. God doesn't discipline slaves, He disciplines sons.

God's discipline is training, not punishment

The Greek word for discipline (paideia) means child-training, not just rebuke. Discipline forms character, not just behavior. Orphans interpret discipline as rejection; sons interpret it as investment.

"Now no chastening seems to be joyful for the present, but painful; nevertheless, afterward it yields the peaceable fruit of righteousness to those who have been trained by it." Hebrews 12:11, NKJV

This verse anchors an important truth in the journey of sonship: correction is not rejection. It is refinement.

Discipline is not proof of distance from the Father; it is evidence of belonging to Him. Hebrews 12 reminds us that whom the Lord loves, He chastens (v. 6), and this correction is not punitive, but formative. It shapes us, trains us, and matures us into His likeness.

This is critical in breaking the orphan mindset. Orphans interpret discipline as anger, distance, or abandonment. Sons interpret discipline as care, attention, and preparation.

God is not punishing us, He is parenting us.

Just as Jesus was made perfect through sufferings (Hebrews 2:10), we too are trained by what we endure. This verse does not glorify pain, it glorifies the outcome: the peaceable fruit of righteousness. In other words, the discipline of God produces harmony, right-standing, alignment, and maturity in those who are willing to be trained.

Notice the key phrase: *"to those who have been trained by it."* This implies that some resist it, misinterpret it, or discard its purpose. But to those who embrace it as sons, not as slaves or strangers, the result is transformation.

Discipline without sonship feels like shame.

But discipline with sonship becomes glory.

It is through correction that sons grow. It is through surrender that we are shaped. And it is through training that we are prepared for the glory we've been adopted into. As sons, we don't run from discipline, we submit to it knowing that it is love in action, preparing us for the fullness of our inheritance.

I have to be honest about something that shaped much of my walk with God in earlier years. Because of a rigid and fear-based religious upbringing, I grew up interpreting discipline as judgment. I viewed God's correction through the lens of wrath, not love. Every failure on my part felt like a trigger for His anger. Every trial looked like punishment.

I didn't see a loving Father; I saw a stern Judge with a short temper and a long list of my shortcomings.

When things went wrong, I often thought: *"I must have disappointed Him again."* When I faced hard seasons, my first question was never, *"Lord, what are you teaching me?"*, it was, *"What did I do wrong?"*

The fear of discipline kept me from drawing near. Instead of running to the Father, I tried to fix myself first. I didn't understand that discipline is not the withdrawal of love, it is the expression of it.

The writer of Hebrews doesn't just say, *"Endure chastening."* He says, *"God deals with you as sons."* (Hebrews 12:7) That hit me one day like a tidal wave of grace. The pain I was so afraid of wasn't proof of God's absence, it was evidence of His fatherhood. He wasn't angry at me. He was training me. Loving me. Investing in me.

I realized that fear had given me the wrong definition of discipline. I thought it was divine disappointment. But it was divine devotion.

The correction I used to dread, I now value, because I know it's forming the image of the Son in me. It's not rejection. It's refinement. It's not shame. It's shaping.

"Blessed is the man whom You discipline, O LORD, and whom You teach out of Your law..." Psalm 94:12, ESV

I'm learning not to flinch when correction comes. I'm learning to say, *"Thank You, Father,"* not because the process is easy, but because I finally know where it's coming from, and what it's producing.

His discipline no longer sends me running from Him, it draws me closer. Because now, I know I'm being fathered.

Orphan response vs. Son response to correction

Orphan Mentality	Son Mentality
Hides in shame	Comes closer in humility
Resists correction	Receives correction
Feels rejected	Feels refined
Runs from discipline	Learns from discipline
Tries to prove worth	Trusts in placement

Even Jesus, though sinless, experienced growth through discipline.

"Though He was a Son, yet He learned obedience by the things which He suffered." – Hebrews 5:8 (NKJV)

He was not corrected for wrong but prepared for reign. Suffering refined His obedience, not His identity. Sonship does not exempt us from pain, it gives pain purpose.

Discipline positions you for your inheritance

"If children, then heirs…" – Romans 8:17 (NKJV)

Discipline is part of how the Father qualifies you to carry what's His. **Immaturity mishandles inheritance.**

The prodigal son wanted inheritance before maturity. The Father gave it, but immaturity wasted it. A son must mature before he inherits fully.

Discipline deepens trust and honor

"We have had human fathers who corrected us… Shall we not much more readily be in subjection to the Father of spirits and live?" – Hebrews 12:9 (NKJV)

God's discipline should lead to greater intimacy, not fear. The fear of the Lord is not dread; it is deep reverence born of love.

Discipline positions you to disciple others

"Make straight paths for your feet, so that what is lame may not be dislocated, but rather be healed." – Hebrews 12:13 (NKJV)

God's discipline in you becomes wisdom for others. Sons become fathers who discipline with grace, not domination. Correction becomes a culture of honor and healing.

The Mark of Sons Is Not Perfection, It's Correction

The discipline of God is not a mark of rejection; it is the unmistakable proof of sonship. Hell cannot counterfeit it,

81

and religion cannot understand it. Correction is not condemnation, it is covenant in action. It is how the Father hands His sons a mirror and says, *"I love you too much to let you live beneath who you are."*

Discipline is not about what you've done wrong, it's about who you're becoming. It's heaven refusing to let earth define you. It's love that won't leave you where shame and fear tried to bury you.

The world punishes to shame; the Father corrects to restore. His discipline doesn't reduce your value, it reveals it.

Only sons are corrected. Slaves are managed. Orphans are ignored. But sons are trained, because sons have destiny.

This isn't about behavior modification. This is about glory. This isn't about getting better. This is about growing brighter.

"For whom the Lord loves He disciplines..." (Hebrews 12:6).

Not punishes. Not crushes. Not abandons.

Disciplines. Shapes. Sharpens. Prepares.

If you're in the fire, it's not because you're forsaken, it's because you're being forged. The cross wasn't the end of Jesus, it was the crown. Likewise, your correction is not your disqualification, it's your confirmation.

You are being fathered into glory.

So stop resisting the hand that's molding you. Stop fearing the voice that corrects you. Stop shrinking back from the God who calls you His own.

This is not wrath.

This is not rejection.

This is love.

This is legacy.

This is sonship.

You're not being punished.

You're being prepared.

Because sons carry the weight of the Father's name—and the world is waiting for the sons of God to be revealed.

Reflection Questions

1. How have you historically viewed God's discipline, as punishment or preparation?

_____

_____

_____

_____

2. What area of your life has God lovingly corrected, and what was the result?

_____

_____

_____

3. Do you run from correction or lean into it?

_____

_____

_____

4. How does Jesus' example of obedience through suffering encourage you?

_____

_____

_____

_____

_____

5. How can you help create a culture of loving correction in your family or church?

_____

_____

_____

_____

_____

_____

6. In what ways has your upbringing or past religious environment shaped how you respond to God's discipline?

_____

_____

_____

_____

_____

_____

7. What would change if you truly believed that God's correction is confirmation of your sonship, not a sign of failure?

_____

_____

_____

_____

_____

NOTES

CHAPTER 6
Inheritance and Legacy

"The Spirit Himself bears witness with our spirit that we are children of God, and if children, then heirs, heirs of God and joint heirs with Christ…"
– Romans 8:16–17 (NKJV)

Inheritance begins with identity

You inherit because of who you are, not what you've done. God doesn't give rewards to sons, He gives inheritance. Orphans work for approval. Sons receive because they belong. Because they belong to the Father, sons live from provision, not production.

"Blessed be the God… who has blessed us with every spiritual blessing in the heavenly places in Christ." – Ephesians 1:3

Legacy flows from inheritance

Inheritance is what you receive. Legacy is what you leave behind. Every son eventually becomes a father.

You don't just receive something, you become someone who represents the Father.

Inheritance is not just future it is now

"Son, you are always with me, and all that I have is yours."
– Luke 15:31 (NKJV)

Inheritance is not just heaven when you die; it's access to the Father's resources now. Many live like spiritual beggars when they're seated at the table. See yourself as a co-heir and steward, not a servant.

Sons carry culture, not just covenant

"He made known His ways to Moses, His acts to the children of Israel." – Psalm 103:7

Sons receive the **ways** of the Father, not just His **works**. Inheritance includes wisdom, values, and language. Some examples are honor instead of control, faith instead of fear, rest instead of striving, holiness as identity.

The orphans trap is wasting inheritance

"Not many days after, the younger son gathered all… and wasted his possessions…" – Luke 15:13

Orphans demand access without maturity. Inheritance without identity leads to loss. The Father restores the prodigal to heart, not just the house.

Sons who understand inheritance release legacy

"A good man leaves an inheritance to his children's children…" – Proverbs 13:22

You are not just carrying something, you are building something. The legacy of a son becomes the foundation for future generations. You aren't just called to end cycles, you're called to start Kingdom ones.

Joint heirs with Christ

"Heirs of God and joint heirs with Christ..." – Romans 8:17

Jesus shares His inheritance with us, not just His throne, but His heart. To be a joint heir means we are invited into fellowship, responsibility, and reign.

Though we often speak of doing the will of God, we must also understand a deeper truth: we are in His will. According to Hebrews 9:16–17, *"For where there is a testament, there must also of necessity be the death of the testator. For a testament is in force after men are dead..."* (NKJV).

A will, or testament, is not about what we do to earn something, it is about what was written and made secure by the death of another.

We are not striving to qualify ourselves into God's inheritance; we are receiving what Christ has secured. Jesus, the Testator, did not merely die for sin, He died to enact a divine will. That will includes you.

You were written in, not by your works or your righteousness, but by the Father's choosing and the Son's obedience. You are not just doing God's will; you are living from the reality that you are in His will.

Inheritance, then, is not the result of performance, it is the outcome of position. The Father willed it. The Son died to ratify it. And the Spirit was given to seal it.

"In Him you also trusted...you were sealed with the Holy Spirit of promise, who is the guarantee of our inheritance..." (Ephesians 1:13–14, NKJV).

The Holy Spirit is not a vague comforter; He is the legal seal on your inheritance. His presence is your down payment, your first taste of what is fully yours in the Kingdom. When you walk in step with the Spirit, you are walking in the full assurance that you are not disqualified, not overlooked, you are a son in the will.

This inheritance, this Kingdom, was not reluctantly granted. Jesus declared, *"It is your Father's good pleasure to give you the Kingdom"* (Luke 12:32, NKJV). The Father is not stingy. He is not hesitant or reluctant. It delights Him to give you what belongs to Him, because sons were always meant to carry what the Father treasures.

And because we are heirs, we are empowered to leave a legacy. We inherit so we can invest. We receive so we can release. We are entrusted with the Kingdom not just to enjoy it but to extend it. The inheritance you've received, righteousness, peace, joy, authority, dominion, is meant to shape what you build and what you leave behind.

Legacy is the visible imprint of invisible inheritance.

When sons walk in their inheritance, the world sees the legacy of the Father.

Reflection Questions

1. How has your view of inheritance shifted as you've embraced sonship?

_____

_____

2. Are there areas where you've acted like a servant or orphan when God has called you an heir?

_____

_____

3. What has God placed in your hands that should become legacy for others?

_____

_____

_____

4. How can you begin to walk in your inheritance today, not just wait for heaven?

_____

_____

5. What kind of culture are you passing on to the next generation?

_____

_____

_____

6. In what ways have you struggled to see yourself as someone who is in God's will—written into His inheritance by grace rather than effort?

_____

_____

_____

_____

_____

7. How does understanding the Holy Spirit as the down payment of your inheritance shift the way you live, pray, and expect from God?

_____

_____

_____

_____

_____

8. What legacy are you building right now that reflects your identity as a son? How are you preparing others to receive and walk in the inheritance of the Kingdom?

_____

_____

_____

_____

_____

NOTES

_____

_____

_____

_____

_____

_____

_____

_____

_____

_____

_____

_____

_____

_____

_____

_____

_____

_____

_____

_____

_____

CHAPTER 7
The Household of Sons

"You are no longer strangers and foreigners, but fellow citizens with the saints and members of the household of God." – Ephesians 2:19 (NKJV)

God never intended for sons to grow alone

Sonship is both personal and corporate. God places sons in family, not just in faith. The first context for Adam's sonship was a garden and a relationship (Eve).

"God sets the solitary in families…" – Psalm 68:6

The Kingdom is a household, not a hierarchy

"In My Father's house are many rooms…" – John 14:2

Religion builds institutions. The Kingdom builds families. Every son belongs in a house, not just in a ministry. The Father is not building a business, He's building a family.

That simple contrast reveals a monumental difference in purpose and design. Religion often concerns itself with systems, rules to manage, programs to maintain, roles to fill. It builds tall structures with rigid ladders, where value is often determined by performance and proximity to leadership. In such environments, people may function, but they rarely flourish. They may serve faithfully but live quietly disconnected, like tenants in a corporation rather than sons in a home.

But the Kingdom of God does not operate this way.

The Father is not building a business, He's building a family. And that family is made up of sons and daughters, not employees or spiritual day laborers. Ministries may have departments, titles, and rosters, but the Kingdom has tables, robes, and rings. Ministries have checklists. The Kingdom has covenants.

Every son belongs in a house, not just in a ministry. Ministry is what we do, but family is where we are known. Many serve in churches faithfully for years without ever feeling like they belong to a household. They know the pastor but not the Father. They know the vision but not the embrace. They carry titles yet feel like orphans in the back room of a large estate.

But God has always desired something more intimate. From the beginning, His design was a household, not just a hierarchy. In Ephesians 2:19, Paul reminds us: *"Now, therefore, you are no longer strangers and foreigners, but fellow citizens with the saints and members of the household of God."* Sons don't just serve, they dwell. They carry inheritance. They multiply legacy. And they bring others into the house, not just the organization.

This is why the restoration of sonship is not a theological novelty; it is the blueprint for the Church. Without sons, we're left with systems. Without fathers, we're left with functionaries. But where sonship is restored, the household is awakened, and the Father's heart becomes the center of everything we do.

From servants to sons in the house

"A slave does not abide in the house forever, but a son abides forever." – John 8:35 (NKJV)

Servant's work for a place. Sons live from a place. That simple shift in mindset determines whether we live for approval or from acceptance. A servant labors with uncertainty, unsure if he's earned enough to stay. A son, however, serves from assurance, he knows he belongs.

Many believers serve with the mindset of a guest, never fully believing the house is theirs. They tiptoe through their spiritual life as if they're on borrowed ground, constantly evaluating whether they've prayed enough, performed enough, or behaved well enough to remain in favor. They volunteer faithfully, tithe consistently, and attend diligently, but deep down, they feel like outsiders. They are in the house, but not at home.

But Jesus didn't die to make us guests in the Father's house, He died to make us sons.

The house was never meant to be a workplace, it was meant to be a dwelling place. Sons don't live on edge, wondering if they'll be dismissed. They walk confidently, knowing they're wanted. They serve, yes, but their service flows from security, not striving.

The tragedy is that many churches have become filled with high-performing servants who've never received the robe of sonship. They attend the feast but sit at the edge of the table. They are faithful, but fearful, afraid to ask, afraid to rest, afraid to fully receive.

But the Father is calling His children home, not just into the building, but into the "belovedness" of their place. Not just into ministry, but into the household. Not just into function, but into family.

Until this revelation penetrates the heart, believers will continue to operate like employees hoping for a bonus instead of heirs walking in abundance.

This statement from Jesus reveals a profound Kingdom principle: A slave may work in the house but doesn't belong to it. A son abides, he belongs, inherits, and remains.

When we look at the life of David, we see a striking fulfillment of this truth. Long before he sat on a throne, David lived with the heart of a son, not a slave. He wasn't just in the house, he belonged to it.

And this is likely why God called him *"a man after My own heart"*, even while he was still just a boy.

1 Samuel 13:14 *"The Lord has sought for Himself a man after His own heart..."*

This was spoken of David before he was ever crowned king, and likely while he was still tending sheep, young, unseen, and uncelebrated.

God wasn't looking at his resume, strength, or age. He was looking at his alignment, because alignment reveals identity. In Kingdom terms God doesn't call us by **where** we are, but by **who** we are.

Just as He called Jeremiah a prophet before he was born (Jer. 1:5), Gideon a mighty man of valor while he was hiding

(Judg. 6:12), He called David a man, even as a boy, because he was already a son.

Sonship before the throne

David exemplified sonship before he ever held a crown.

He Lived in the **Presence**, Not Just in **Performance**

"One thing I have desired… that I may dwell in the house of the Lord all the days of my life…" (Ps. 27:4)

David longed to dwell, not just serve. He didn't perform to be seen; he worshiped to be near. He Was prophetic about God as Father

"He shall cry to Me, 'You are my Father, My God, and the rock of my salvation." (Ps. 89:26)

Even under the Old Covenant, where "Father" was rarely used, David reached into New Covenant language, revealing his sonship consciousness.

He was promised a perpetual house

"I will establish his kingdom… I will be his Father, and he shall be My son." (2 Sam. 7:12–14)

God promised to build David a house, not just a throne, because David lived as a son, not just a servant. And this would ultimately point to Jesus, the Son of David.

He Honored Authority Like a Son

Though Saul was rejected, David refused to dishonor him, because a true son doesn't take by force what only the Father can give by promise.

Abba and paternity: two dimensions of sonship

"A slave does not abide in the house forever, but a son abides forever." (John 8:35)

Jesus introduces a contrast; slaves are present by duty, but sons remain by belonging.

This is echoed in the language of sonship. "Abba" (Aramaic) is the intimate cry, like "Papa" or "Daddy." "Pater" (Greek) is the legal authority, the Father of a household.

David knew both: He wept in intimacy (Abba), singing psalms in hidden places. He walked in confidence (Pater), knowing the Lord would establish him. David was a son.

He didn't just visit God's house, he abided in it. That's why he could declare:

"I will dwell in the house of the Lord forever." (Psalm 23:6)

Honor is the culture of His house

"Honor all people. Love the brotherhood. Fear God. Honor the king." – 1 Peter 2:17

Sons thrive in cultures of honor. Honor makes room for difference without division and protects relationships even

100

when correction is needed. Son's honor fathers. Fathers affirm sons. Brothers celebrate one another.

Accountability and authority grow in family

Family is the training ground for maturity. In the Kingdom of God, authority is not about control, and accountability is not about punishment. Both are rooted in relationship, not rigid legalism. Accountability is Relational, Not Legalistic

In a legalistic system accountability is enforced from the outside. Rules govern behavior, but rarely transform the heart. Fear of punishment replaces love for truth.

In a Kingdom family accountability flows from trust and shared identity. It's about being known, corrected, and loved into maturity. Sons submit not because they fear man, but because they honor the Father.

Hebrews 13:17 (NKJV): *"Obey those who rule over you, and be submissive, for they watch out for your souls, as those who must give account. Let them do so with joy and not with grief, for that would be unprofitable for you."*

Breakdown and Kingdom Insight:

"Obey those who rule over you…"

"Rule" here is from the Greek hēgeomai — which means to lead, guide, or go before, not dominate. True spiritual leadership is servant leadership, it's modeled by example, not enforced by threat. In family, this looks like fathers and mothers guiding sons and daughters, not taskmasters commanding slaves.

101

"...be submissive..." Submission (hypeikō) is voluntary yielding, not forced compliance. It implies a trusting relationship, the kind that only grows in the context of family. Sons submit to fathers because they believe in their love and wisdom, not because they fear consequences.

"...for they watch out for your souls..." This is shepherding language, intimate, protective, and deeply relational. True leaders in the Kingdom care for souls, not just manage behavior. Like shepherds, they stand guard against spiritual threats, because they see those under them as family, not followers.

"...as those who must give account." Authority in the Kingdom is always accountable upward, no one leads without being led. This keeps leadership humble, and servant hearted. Fathers and leaders will answer to God the Father, not just for how they led, but how they loved.

"Let them do so with joy and not with grief..." Healthy family leadership is a joy, when those being led are responsive, honoring, and growing When sons rebel or resist, it causes grief, not because of pride, but because of love and shared responsibility.

Kingdom family training ground

In a true spiritual family authority is fatherly. It develops, disciplines, and dignifies. Accountability is brotherly, it restores, reminds, and refines. There's room to fail forward, to learn, to grow, and to mature, because family is relationally safe and spiritually strong.

Even Jesus submitted to earthly parents (Luke 2:51), and to His heavenly Father, not out of obligation, but out of love, honor, and alignment.

Practical application

Leaders should not demand authority but cultivate trust and be accountable yourself. **Sons** do not resist correction but see it as a sign you're loved enough to be formed. And **churches** should replace hierarchical systems with relational families, fathering and forming people into maturity.

In the Kingdom, authority isn't about control, it's about covering. It isn't about exposure, it's about development. Both flourish best in the safety and structure of spiritual family.

Every house has a culture to be shaped and shared

Sons preserve the values of the house, speak the language of the house, and serve the vision of the house, not as slaves, but as stakeholders.

This reflects the core of biblical sonship: a son carries the heart, honor, and heritage of his father's house. He doesn't just represent it, he extends it.

Malachi 1:6 (NKJV): *"A son honors his father, and a servant his master. If then I am the Father, where is My honor? And if I am a Master, where is My reverence?" says the Lord of hosts...*

This verse reveals that God expects sons to honor and to reflect the values, character, and weight of the Father's name, which is the standard of His household. Israel's failure to honor God wasn't just disobedience, it was a break in sonship. When Israel treated God like a taskmaster instead of a Father, they lost the language of honor.

Babylon: a system that targeted sons

Daniel 1:3–4 Nebuchadnezzar commanded: *"Bring some of the children of Israel and some of the king's descendants and some of the nobles, young men in whom there was no blemish... and whom they might teach the language and literature of the Chaldeans."*

He wasn't just selecting random captives, he was after the sons of royalty, the princes, the future of the house.

What did Babylon try to change?

Their Identity – Daniel, Hananiah, Mishael, and Azariah were all given new Babylonian names (Belteshazzar, Shadrach, Meshach, Abed-Nego) — a direct assault on their God-given identity.

Their Language – They were taught the language of the Chaldeans, not to communicate better, but to erase the dialect of Zion, the language of their spiritual house.

Their Diet – They were commanded to eat the king's food, which would violate covenant law, changing their appetite and ultimately, their loyalty.

Their Allegiance – Ultimately, Babylon's goal was to reprogram sons into servants, to sever them from their Father's house, values, and vision.

The agenda of Babylon was not simply to enslave Israel, it was to redefine the royal sons who had been raised in covenant. By changing their names, retraining their language, reshaping their appetites, and redirecting their allegiance, Babylon attempted to reprogram sons into cultural servants. Likewise, the spirit of religion threatens the identity of the Household of Sons.

It does not always come with chains, but often with compromise, replacing intimacy with structure, and inheritance with obligation. Religion subtly dismantles the foundations of sonship by redefining identity through function, silencing the language of the Spirit, feeding performance over presence, and demanding allegiance to systems instead of to the Father.

In doing so, it attempts to turn sons into servants of a structure rather than stakeholders in a family. But in the true Household of Sons, identity flows from the Father, language is born of intimacy, appetite is shaped by truth, and loyalty is secured in love.

Like Daniel and his companions, sons who remain anchored in the values of the house can resist the pressures of Babylon and refuse to be assimilated. This chapter is a call back to the house, to live, speak, and serve not as slaves, but as sons who abide.

Sons in exile: preserving the house in a foreign land

Daniel and his companions resisted the Babylonian program not as rebels, but as sons who remembered their Father. They honored God over kings, risking their lives rather than defiling their covenant (Dan. 1:8).

Preserved the language of prayer and worship, even when forbidden (Dan. 6:10). They **served** in Babylon, but never **became** Babylonian.

They didn't just survive exile, they preserved the values of the Kingdom, carried the language of the house, and served God's vision through excellence and loyalty.

Connection to Malachi 1:6

Israel lost its sonship posture in the temple, but Daniel preserved it in Babylon. The issue wasn't location, it was identity and honor. Babylon (Religion based in confusion and mixture) wants sons to forget whose house they came from.

God seeks sons who will honor Him even in foreign systems, preserving the culture of His Kingdom.

Kingdom Application

Sons honor the Father, even in unfamiliar territory. They preserve the language, values, and integrity of the Kingdom. They serve the Father's vision, not for position, but for inheritance.

Babylon Still Speaks:

Today's Babylon (religious systems) still try to rename, retrain, and reassign sons. But the true test of sonship is whether we remain faithful to the voice of the Father, or whether we trade our inheritance for cultural acceptance.

When Nebuchadnezzar sought to redefine sons into servants, he was attempting to sever their Kingdom DNA. But sons like Daniel stood firm, not because of rebellion, but because of honor. They carried their Father's house into Babylon, proving that a son honors even in exile.

Sons make room for other sons

In the Father's house, no one needs to compete. The older brother in Luke 15 missed this, he served without intimacy and resented restoration. Sons must celebrate when prodigals return and make room for brothers in the house.

Reflection Questions

1. Do you see yourself as a son in the house or as a servant trying to earn a place?

_____

_____

_____

2. How can you actively contribute to the culture of honor in your church or spiritual family?

_____

_____

_____

_____

_____

3. Are there relationships in your 'household of faith' that need healing or deeper covenant?

_____

_____

_____

4. Do you find yourself competing with others or celebrating them?

_____

_____

_____

5. What does being 'planted in the house of the Lord' look like for you practically?

_____

_____

_____

_____

_____

_____

6. Have you ever felt like religion attempted to reidentify you as a servant?

_____

_____

_____

_____

_____

_____

7. How are you applying the principle of sonship in your life relative to that reidentification?

_____

_____

_____

_____

_____

_____

CHRISTOPHER TURNEY

NOTES

110

CHAPTER 8
From servants to sons

"Therefore you are no longer a slave but a son, and if a son, then an heir of God through Christ."
– Galatians 4:7 (NKJV)

God uses servanthood, but He never desire slaves

Throughout Scripture, faithful men like Moses were called servants of the Lord, and honored as such. But when Jesus appeared, He came not as another servant, but as the Son, revealing a higher order of relationship.

"God is not looking for slaves to serve Him, but sons to know Him."

— Jack Frost, from 'Experiencing Father's Embrace'

Servants may be entrusted with assignments, but sons are entrusted with the house. As Jesus Himself declared,

"The servant does not remain in the house forever, but a son remains forever" (John 8:35).

This statement wasn't just theological, it was relational. It exposed the limitations of religious servitude and unveiled the Father's true desire: a family, not a workforce. Jesus didn't die to recruit laborers. He died to reconcile sons. When He said,

"I go to prepare a place for you" (John 14:2)

He wasn't just referring to heaven, He was revealing the Father's intent to make room for us in His presence. From Eden to the New Jerusalem, God's heart has remained the same: to dwell with sons.

At the end of all things, this desire is fulfilled when He declares in Revelation 21:3,

"Behold, the dwelling place of God is with men."

The story of redemption is the story of God calling His people out of servanthood and into sonship, from laborers in His field to heirs in His house

Religion produces servants; revelation produces sons

"Religion is man's attempt to reach God; sonship is God's success in reaching man." — Author Unknown

Servants obey out of fear; sons obey out of love. A servant's motivation is to earn favor. A son's motivation is to express identity.

"… I no longer call you servants…" – John 15:15
For years, I lived with a servant mindset. I wouldn't have called it that at the time, it felt spiritual, even noble. I just wanted to please God. My deepest desire was to one day hear those sacred words: *"Well done, good and faithful servant."* That phrase rang in my ears like a prize I had to earn. And so I served, fervently, tirelessly, and sacrificially. I labored in ministry, watched over people, and carried the weight of responsibility on my shoulders. But behind the

sincerity of my service was a subtle but heavy fear: What if I'm not doing enough? What if He's not pleased with me?

I didn't yet know that my sonship pleased Him more than my service ever could.

Before Jesus ever preached a sermon, healed the sick, cast out a demon, or fed the hungry, the Father publicly affirmed Him:

"This is My beloved Son, in whom I am well pleased" (Matthew 3:17, NKJV).

This wasn't a reward for a job well done. It was an affirmation of identity, of shared likeness. What pleased the Father wasn't Jesus' performance; it was His personhood. The Father saw Himself in the Son. And that is what pleased Him.

I had missed that for so long. I thought I was serving for love, when I was really serving for approval. I was afraid of disappointing Him. My whole life became an offering of effort, hoping to earn a smile from Heaven. But sons don't earn smiles, they inherit them. The Father's approval isn't something to achieve; it's something to receive.

The turning point for me was realizing that He was never asking for more performance, He was waiting for more proximity. I had confused pleasing Him with appeasing Him. I approached God like a worker clocking in at a job site, not a son walking into his Father's house. I was a servant in the Kingdom, but a stranger to the household.

But sonship doesn't start with serving; it starts with seeing. Seeing the Father. Seeing yourself in His eyes. And realizing that the deepest pleasure of Heaven is not found in your accomplishments, but in your identity.

It's not that God rejects service, He redeems it through sonship. In the Kingdom, serving doesn't define identity; identity defines service. Sons still serve, but not to become sons. They serve because they are sons. The posture shifts entirely.

"Servant is what I do, son is who I am"

Again, Galatians 4:7 says it plainly:

"Therefore you are no longer a slave but a son, and if a son, then an heir of God through Christ" (NKJV).

The transition isn't from slavery to independence. It's from slavery to inheritance. From duty to delight. From obligation to overflow. God's goal wasn't to take us out of Egypt just to make us workers in the wilderness. His desire was always to bring us into a house, not just a job.

Jesus makes this transition explicit in John 15:15:

"No longer do I call you servants… but I have called you friends."

He doesn't deny that they were once servants. But He reveals that proximity changes status. And ultimately, love changes the nature of service. Servants work without access to the heart of the master. Friends, and even more so sons, are invited into the will, the wisdom, and the inheritance of the Father.

Romans 8:15–16 deepens this further: *"For you did not receive the spirit of bondage again to fear, but you received the Spirit of adoption by whom we cry out, 'Abba, Father.'"*

Fear-driven service is not Kingdom service. The Spirit we've received doesn't chain us to tasks; it awakens us to family. And the cry of "Abba" is not a theological concept, it's the sound of sons who know they're loved.

The tragedy is how many believers continue to serve with a guest mentality. They work in the house but never feel at home. They operate like renters, grateful to be included but always afraid they'll be asked to leave. But sons? Sons know where the silverware is. Sons open the fridge. Sons don't need permission to come into the living room. Sons belong.

Servants work for a place. Sons live from a place. And that place is the Father's love.

From duty to delight: the shift in intimacy

Servants focus on assignments; sons focus on the Father's heart.

Jesus didn't say, *"I only do what I am assigned."* He said, *"I only do what I see My Father doing."*

"The Father loves the Son, and shows Him all things..." – John 5:20

The prodigals return: two types of servant mindsets

"I am no longer worthy to be called your son. Make me like one of your hired servants." (Luke 15:19, NKJV)

115

This wasn't just a moment of humility, it was a declaration shaped by shame. He was willing to forfeit identity for the sake of survival. But listen again to his request: *"Make me like one of your hired servants."*

The irony is staggering. He believed the Father had power to make him a servant, but not restore him as a son. He recognized authority, but not love. He assumed that the Father would use that authority to relegate him to servanthood rather than restore him to sonship. And that's the tragedy many believers still carry today.

They believe in God's omnipotence, He can heal, deliver, discipline, and bless. But they don't trust His heart as Father. They return to church, to service, to prayer, asking God to *"make them a servant,"* not realizing they were always sons. They reduce divine restoration to a demotion rather than a resurrection.

They know God can, but they don't believe He wants to.

The truth is, the prodigal never stopped being a son. He only stopped believing he was one. And what restored him wasn't better behavior, it was the Father's embrace, robe, ring, and feast. The Father never even let him finish his speech. He cut him off with compassion.

Because the Father was never interested in hiring him, He was waiting to hug him.

And the same is true for you.

God is not merely powerful. He is love. He doesn't want workers more than He wants sons. He doesn't want performance, He wants proximity. The greatest tragedy in the church is not that people don't believe God can do anything, it's that they don't believe He wants them.

Our existence is proof that God wants us.

You didn't create yourself. You didn't initiate your life. You were spoken into being by a Father who desired you before the foundation of the world. The very breath in your lungs testifies that He chose you. You are not an accident, not a burden, not a second thought, you are a desire of God's heart.

You couldn't be here without Him.

He is not merely tolerating you. He is sustaining you. You are here because He willed you into being. That means your existence is an echo of His desire.

That is what makes the orphan spirit such a cruel deception. It blinds sons into thinking they must earn what was always freely given. It convinces daughters that their belonging must be proven when it was established by creation. But here is the truth that breaks that lie:

Before you ever did anything for Him, He wanted you.

Not as a servant. Not as a hired worker. As a son.

Again, Jesus, before He ever preached a sermon or performed a miracle, was affirmed by the voice of the Father:

"This is My beloved Son, in whom I am well pleased." (Matthew 3:17, NKJV)

Why? Because what pleased the Father wasn't Jesus' ministry. It was that the Father saw Himself in the Son. The Father delights in likeness. And when He looks at you, clothed in Christ, sealed by the Spirit, He sees His own image restored.

You don't have to work to get God to want you. You wouldn't be here if He didn't. The invitation isn't to earn His affection, it's to receive it.

But you were never created to work for God's love. You were created to live from it. The story is called the parable of the Prodigal son, however this parable is not about one son but two.

In the Parable of the Prodigal Son (Luke 15:11–32), the younger brother had mindset of self-degradation

"I am no longer worthy to be called your son. Make me like one of your hired servants." (v.19)

After squandering his inheritance, the younger son returns not to reclaim sonship, but to negotiate servanthood. He assumes that his failure disqualified his identity, and so he tries to earn back proximity through performance.

This is the penance mindset, the belief that restoration comes by labor, not by love. He sees the Father as a master who must be appeased, not as a Father who still desires him.

He is willing to be in the house, but only as one that would serve the table, not sit at the table. This is the mindset of those who confuse forgiveness with probation, thinking, *"If I work hard enough, maybe I'll be accepted again."*

The older brother had the mindset of entitlement,

"All these years I've been serving you… yet you never gave me a young goat." (v.29)

While the younger brother tried to earn love through return, the older brother expected reward through religious loyalty. He didn't rebel outwardly, but inwardly, he too was estranged, serving without joy, staying without intimacy.

His complaint revealed that he saw himself more as an employee than a son. He didn't rejoice in his brother's return because he never really understood the Father's heart, he had lived by the rules, but never embraced the relationship.

When the older brother was found, he was in the servants' field not the Father's house.

Luke 15:25 – *"Now his older son was in the field…"*

This small detail carries a major revelation. Though he never left physically, the older son had also distanced himself from the father relationally.

The servants field: a picture of misplaced identity

The field was where servants labored, not where sons fellowshipped. He was serving, but not celebrating. He was faithful, but not free. He was in the Father's domain, but not in the Father's presence.

His identity had been shaped by duty, not delight.

Servanthood in the name of loyalty

The older brother believed that staying and working hard earned him favor. Yet his bitterness reveals that he saw himself more as an unrewarded worker than a beloved son:

"All these years I've been serving you…" (v.29)

He was physically near, but spiritually detached, living more like a hired servant than a household heir.

He was serving in the field while there was a feast on the table

While the Father was throwing a celebration for restoration, the older son was toiling outside the joy of the house. This paints a picture of many in the Church today, laboring in ministry, faithfulness, or tradition, but disconnected from the intimacy of the Father's heart.

You can be in the field and still far from the Father. The field may look like faithfulness, but if it lacks fellowship, it's a sign that sonship has been replaced by servanthood.

I know this because I lived it.

There was a season in my life where I wouldn't have said it out loud, but deep down, I felt that my faithfulness had earned me a certain standing with God. I had given, labored, served, and sacrificed. I had prayed until I was empty and poured into others until I was dry. I didn't ask for much, but when I saw others being blessed, advancing, or celebrated, especially those I didn't feel had done as much, I felt something rise in me. Not always jealousy. Sometimes confusion. Sometimes frustration.

"God, haven't You seen what I've done? Don't You remember my faithfulness?"

Without realizing it, I had slipped into the shoes of the elder brother in Luke 15. I had stayed in the house. I had done the work. But I was living like a servant, not a son.

My heart had started to measure love by labor. And in doing so, I had missed the Father's heart altogether. But here's what I've come to learn, something I wish I had known sooner:

You are not in Christ life because of your usefulness. You are in His heart because of your likeness.

The Father doesn't love you for what you do. He loves you because He sees Himself in you. Your very existence is the evidence that you were wanted, planned, and formed in love. You're not an afterthought or an accident. You were always His idea.

You were never just invited to serve; you were born to belong.

This is the mindset of those who believe their years of service earn them privileges in the Kingdom, often leading to comparison, resentment, and pride.

Both brothers lived under a system of wages, not relationship

Though they took different paths, both sons fell into the same trap. One tried to work his way back in through guilt. The other tried to earn blessing through effort.

Neither saw the inheritance of relationship, that sonship is not based on wages, but on belonging. The Father's response to both is revealing:

To the younger the father said *"Bring out the best robe… this son of mine was dead and is alive again."* (v.22–24)

To the older he said *"All that I have is yours… you are always with me."* (v.31)

Both sons were invited not just into the house, but into the heart of the Father. One didn't feel worthy to be in the house, the other chose to be in the field. Both were sons that settled to be servants!

In the household of sons, neither failure nor performance determines your identity.

You don't work your way in, you are born again into the family. Servants think in terms of transactions. Sons live in the reality of relationship.

"Bring out the best robe… put a ring on his hand… shoes on his feet…" – Luke 15:22

The Father didn't correct the son's behavior; He restored his identity. When God restores, He does not reduce you to a role, He returns you to a relationship.

When the prodigal son returned, rehearsing his speech of unworthiness and hoping for the role of a servant, the Father did something shocking: He interrupted the confession and initiated restoration. He didn't respond with rebuke, rules, or even a lesson. Instead, He responded with robes, rings, and restoration.

The robe: covering his condition

The Father said, "Bring out the best robe." This wasn't just a fresh change of clothes, it was a symbol of honor, identity, and dignity.

The robe covered the son's filth and shame, not by denial, but by grace. In Scripture, robes often represent righteousness and royalty (Isaiah 61:10).

The Father doesn't dress sons based on where they've been but based on who they are to Him.

The ring: restoring authority

The ring symbolized authority, access, and trust. In ancient culture, a signet ring bore the family seal, it meant you carried the name and backing of the house.

The son didn't earn his way back into that kind of trust, it was granted immediately, because the Father wasn't restoring an employee; He was reaffirming a son.

God doesn't just forgive your past, He entrusts you again, because your identity was never revoked.

The shoes; releasing destiny

In biblical times, slaves were barefoot, but sons wore shoes. By putting sandals on his feet, the Father was saying:

"You are not returning as a servant at the door, you are walking again as a son in this house."

The shoes symbolize a walk renewed, restored purpose, movement, and belonging. God doesn't just welcome you home , He equips you to walk forward in purpose.

The Fathers heart

Notice, the Father never addressed the son's sin directly. Why?

Because true transformation flows not from correction, but from connection. He didn't lower the son to a servant role to teach him humility. He lifted him back into relationship, knowing that identity would realign everything else.

The Father's heart is not behavior modification, it's identity restoration. When God restores, He doesn't reduce you to a role. He restores you to relationship, re-robes you with honor, re-rings you with authority, and re-shoes you with destiny.

That's the transition from servants to sons, and that's the Father's heart.

"But you have received the Spirit of adoption…" – Romans 8:15

Sonship doesn't eliminate service, it redeems it.

In the Kingdom, sons still serve, but the spirit in which they serve is entirely different. Servants serve to be seen or accepted; sons serve because they are already secure and loved.

Romans 8:15 reminds us that we did not receive a spirit of bondage again to fear, that's the servant mindset: working out of fear, pressure, or performance. Instead, we received the Spirit of adoption, which awakens our hearts to cry "Abba, Father."

This Spirit changes everything. It reorients our motivation from earning to expressing. It transforms our work from obligation to overflow. It turns our hands from tools of slavery into acts of love and worship.

Sons don't serve for acceptance; they serve from it. Sons don't work to gain the Father's heart, they work because they already have it.

Jesus the perfect model

Philippians 2:7 tells us Jesus took on the form of a servant, yet He never stopped being the Son.

This is critical. He didn't come as a slave trying to impress the Father, He came as a Son, fully submitted, expressing the Father's heart through humility.

Even in servanthood, His sonship defined Him. Washing feet wasn't beneath Him, it revealed His royalty.

How Did Washing Feet Reveal His Royalty?

Washing feet was the lowliest task in ancient Near Eastern culture, typically done by the lowest-ranking servant in the household. So, when Jesus, the Son of God and rightful King, got down and washed His disciples' feet (John 13:3–5), He wasn't abandoning His royal identity, He was revealing the true nature of it.

True Royalty Expresses Itself in Humility

"Jesus, knowing that the Father had given all things into His hands... rose from supper... and began to wash the disciples' feet." — John 13:3–5

John is careful to note that Jesus knew who He was, He knew He had all things, that He had come from God and was going back to God. In other words, His act of humility wasn't insecurity, it flowed from confidence in His identity as the Son.

In the Kingdom, humility isn't the absence of royalty, it is its highest expression.

Earthly kings assert power.

Heaven's King stoops in love.

He was following His Father

"I only do what I see My Father doing..."
— John 5:19

Jesus showed us that royalty in the Father's house is marked by service, not status. He wasn't just washing feet; He was modeling the culture of the call to sonship, where greatness is expressed through sacrificial love.

"Whoever desires to become great among you, let him be your servant." (Matt. 20:26)

In Kingdom culture, the greatest is not the one with the throne, it's the one with the towel. He Was reversing the curse of fallen dominion

When Adam fell, dominion became domination. But Jesus, the last Adam, redefined dominion through servant-hearted

126

rulership. Washing feet was not a denial of His authority, it was the redeeming of it.

He was showing that real authority is safe when it flows from love. He was crowning His disciples with purpose When He finished, He said:

"I have given you an example, that you should do as I have done to you." (John 13:15)

Only a true King can commission others with His royal standard. He wasn't just cleaning their feet; He was qualifying them to carry His Kingdom.

By washing them, He marked them as servant-kings, just like Him. Jesus washing feet was not the act of a slave, it was the act of a secure Son.

It didn't diminish His royalty. It displayed it in its most glorious form. Love stooping low, because it reigns from above.

Obedience unto death wasn't weakness, it was willing surrender from love. Jesus didn't serve to gain a crown; He served because He already had a place in the house.

THE DIFFERENCE IN SPIRIT

Servant Mindset	Sonship Spirit
Works to earn approval	Works from secure identity
Driven by fear or obligation	Motivated by love

Seeks recognition or reward	Delights in the Father's pleasure
Competes for favor	Carries family values
Performs for position	Serves from relationship

When the Spirit of sonship fills the heart, it redeems service, not by removing it, but by purifying it. Sons become the most faithful servants not because they're forced to serve, but because they're free to love.

In the call to sonship, service is not lost, it's reimagined through the lens of intimacy, inheritance, and alignment.

In the Kingdom, sons serve, but not to earn approval. They serve because they are loved, trusted, and established in the house.

And because they know they are sons, their service becomes an expression of love, not a condition of belonging.

From working for to working with

"We are God's fellow workers…" – 1 Corinthians 3:9

Sons don't work for the Father like employees. They work with the Father as heirs. We've been invited into co-laboring, where rest, trust, and joy fuel action.

Reflection Questions

1. In what ways have you been serving God from a servant mindset instead of a son's heart?

_____

_____

_____

2. Which brother (younger or older) in Luke 15 do you relate to most, and why?

_____

_____

_____

3. How does your understanding of identity affect your intimacy with God?

_____

_____

_____

_____

4. Do you find your value in what you do, or who you are in Him?

_____

_____

_____

_____

5. How can you begin to work with God instead of merely for Him?

_____

_____

_____

6. How has your view of servanthood changed in light of sonship?

_____

_____

_____

7. Do I serve to be seen, or because I am secure?

_____

_____

_____

_____

8. Do I define myself more by what I do for God, or by who I am to God?

_____

_____

_____

_____

_____

NOTES

CHAPTER 9
Manifesting Sonship on the Earth

God's plan has never been merely to send messengers, but to manifest sons.

The Kingdom does not advance by the multiplication of ministers alone, it advances by the manifestation of sons. Heaven is not looking for those who are simply authorized to go, but those who are like the One who sends them. It is not enough to be anointed. Saul was anointed. It is not enough to be called. Judas was called. What God longs to send into the world is not just gifted representatives, but image-bearers. Sons.

Jesus illustrates this clearly in the parable of the vineyard (Matthew 21:33–41). The owner of the vineyard sent servants first, but they were beaten, rejected, and killed. Finally, the text says:

"Last of all he sent unto them his son, saying, 'They will reverence my son.'" Matthew 21:37, KJV

This was not a matter of authorization, it was a matter of likeness. He didn't say, *"I will send another agent."* He said, *"I will send my son."* A son carries something more than a title, he carries the heart and image of the father. Sons do not just represent the house, they extend it.

This is why the manifestation of sons is not just a functional act, it is a revelatory one.

CHRISTOPHER TURNEY

Hebrews 1:3 calls Jesus the charaktēr of God, the exact imprint of His nature. The Greek word speaks of an engraving or stamped image, one that bears the full character and essence of the original. When God desired to show the world who He truly was, He did not raise up another prophet.

He sent His Son, One who would not abandon His likeness.

"He who has seen Me has seen the Father."

(John 14:9, NKJV)

This was not metaphor, it was identity. Jesus didn't come to perform like the Father. He came as the very image of the Father. That is the weight of true sonship: the world sees the Father through the Son.

Jesus was not merely another preacher like John in the wilderness. He wasn't just a deliverer like Moses, or a patriarch like Abraham, or a miracle-working prophet like Elijah. He was the only begotten of the Father, full of grace and truth. He was the Son, eternally existent, not created. And when the Word became flesh (John 1:1), the world witnessed the full manifestation of sonship.

"For this purpose the Son of God was manifested, that He might destroy the works of the devil." 1 John 3:8, KJV

Every force that tried to resist Him bowed in submission:

- The waters held Him and obeyed His command.
- The grave had to release Lazarus when He spoke.
- The mud on a blind man's eyes became healing.
- The heavens rolled open at His baptism.
- Demons trembled at His presence.

134

- Death itself was dismantled by His resurrection.

Why? Because creation recognizes not just dominion, but likeness. It wasn't just that He came with authority, it was that He came as the Son. And in Him, the fullness of the Father was pleased to dwell (Colossians 1:19).

Authority without identity is hollow. But Sonship carries the DNA of the Father. When Jesus spoke, creation didn't just hear power; it recognized its Creator's voice expressed through His Son.

When Jesus spoke, creation didn't just hear power, it recognized its Creator's voice expressed through His Son. The wind, the waves, the earth, and even death itself responded, not merely to authority, but to the Word that framed them in the beginning.

This opens a sacred dialogue between time and eternity. From the very beginning, creation was shaped by the voice of God. Hebrews 11:3 tells us, *"By faith we understand that the worlds were framed by the word of God."*

That Word was not simply sound; it was the Son. John declared it plainly: *"In the beginning was the Word... and the Word became flesh and dwelt among us"* (John 1:1,14).

Jesus was not a new idea, He was the eternal expression of God's voice, clothed in human form.

When the Father sent His Son, He didn't send a sermon, He sent His Son as the Seed. The Word entered Mary not just to be received, but to be conceived. She didn't just hear it; she became pregnant with it. And that divine seed, spoken by the Spirit, carried by a woman, was the manifestation of

135

everything God ever said. That is why every Word God speaks does not return void. It is alive, creative, and targeted to finish what it was sent to do.

So, when Jesus said, *"Peace,"* the wind and waves responded, not as strangers, but as children hearing the familiar sound of their Maker. They had heard this voice before. It was the same voice that said, *"Let there be."* When Jesus said, *"Be healed,"* the molecules in a broken body, the dust from which man was formed, recognized the tone that originally shaped their structure.

This is the mystery of manifestation: Jesus didn't just represent the Father, He revealed Him. He didn't just echo Heaven's voice, He was Heaven's voice. And this is what creation groans for even now. Not just for preachers with microphones, but for sons who speak with the resonance of the Father. Sons who aren't just authorized but awakened. Sons who don't just quote Scripture but embody the living Word.

Creation is longing to serve sons again. The earth wants to yield its harvest. The seas long to carry them safely to divine assignments. The dust wants to obey their hands in miracles. The grave is prepared to release what it holds when a son calls with Heaven's voice.

Why? Because sons are not just a voice in the earth, they are His voice. And when that voice is heard again in likeness and love, the world will not just shake, it will respond. Creation itself will find its freedom when sons step forward, clothed not just in gifts, but in the glory of identity.

In recent years, the message of the Kingdom has gained renewed emphasis. The Church is awakening to the reality that we are not here to escape earth, but to reign on it. Kingdom language has rightfully reminded us of our dominion. But we must not stop at dominion, we must return to likeness. For it was to the one who bore God's image and likeness that dominion was entrusted (Genesis 1:26).

Dominion without likeness leads to delusion. It causes people to assume power without intimacy, to try ruling without reflecting. That's what religion does, it teaches people to act like God without knowing Him. But the Kingdom doesn't work that way. Authority is not inherited through calling alone; it flows through identification.

When we try to walk in Kingdom dominion apart from Kingdom sonship, we misrepresent the King. We may speak in His name but not reflect His nature. That's why Jesus wasn't just sent, He was manifested. Because the Father knew: only likeness can truly reign.

The called-out ones, those sent into the earth, must first return to the place of sonship. Dominion flows from identity, not effort. Creation won't respond to titles, platforms, or declarations that lack the aroma of the Father. But when true sons step forward, those who carry the heart, the character, and the likeness of the King, then and only then does the world respond.

Herein lies the call to every believer, not merely to serve, but to manifest. Not merely to go, but to be sent as sons. This manifestation does not begin with ministry, it begins with awakening. We must be awakened to our identity as sons before we ever attempt to extend the Kingdom.

For the Father is not interested in building an empire of workers, but in raising a household of sons.

"For the earnest expectation of the creation eagerly waits for the revealing of the sons of God."
– Romans 8:19 (NKJV)

But the story does not end with Jesus. He was the firstborn among many brethren (Romans 8:29). The manifestation of the Son was not an isolated event, it was the prototype for the manifestation of many sons.

And now…Creation waits

"For the earnest expectation of the creature waiteth for the manifestation of the sons of God."
– Romans 8:19, KJV

This is staggering. All of creation, every particle of dust, every wave of the sea, every blade of grass, is on tiptoe, groaning with anticipation, aching not for another preacher, not for another program, not even for another miracle worker… but for sons.

Creation remembers Eden

It remembers what it was like to respond to a man who walked in the full likeness of God. It remembers the authority Adam carried before the fall. It remembers what it was like to serve the one who bore the image of the Creator without distortion.

The wind, the soil, the sky, and the stars, all of it still echoes with the memory of perfect order. And now, creation groans, not to go back to Eden, but to move forward into the

138

revealing of sons who walk as Christ walked. Sons who bear the image of God, not just in theory, but in reality. Sons who restore order through likeness, not legalism.

This is precisely why Jesus came.

John 3:16 is one of the most quoted verses in Scripture, yet it is often viewed through a narrow lens, as if it's only about individual salvation from sin. But the original Greek offers a deeper perspective. The word "world" in this verse is kosmos, not anthropos (man), nor ge (earth), but kosmos, meaning the entire ordered system of creation, arrangement, and design.

It refers not only to humanity, but to the divine structure of creation, including the harmony of Heaven and Earth under God's rule.

"For God so loved the kosmos…" (John 3:16)

This was not simply an emotional reaction to human failure. It was a divine response to disorder. God loved the order He had created and desired to restore it, not merely by rescuing individuals, but by redeeming the entire structure through the reintroduction of sons. Jesus came to bring alignment, to restore what had been broken in Genesis. The fall disfigured the image, fractured identity, and distorted dominion. But the Son Came, not just to forgive sin, but to reinstall sonship.

When Jesus came, He reestablished the prototype. He didn't only die for man, He lived as man was intended to live. He didn't just save us from judgment, He reintroduced the image. Through His life, death, and resurrection, He reopened the blueprint of Genesis: the likeness of God ruling in love, walking in communion, stewarding creation, and reflecting Heaven.

The love of God in John 3:16 is not just sentimental, it is structural. It is about restoring the framework of the kosmos through the revealing of sons who walk in union with the Father.

And now, creation longs to be governed again, not by fallen man, but by awakened sons. Sons who remember what Adam forgot. Sons who don't reach for the tree of knowledge but walk with the One who is Wisdom. Sons who bring order by their very presence. Not because they command it, but because they carry His image again. The earth does not respond to position. It responds to identity.

"For the creation was subjected to futility, not willingly, but because of Him who subjected it in hope; because the creation itself also will be delivered from the bondage of corruption into the glorious liberty of the children of God."
– Romans 8:20–21, NKJV

Creation was subjected to frustration, placed under a curse, forced to bear the consequences of a fallen steward. But it was done in hope, because a new race of sons would come, born not of Adam, but of Christ. And with their revealing, creation itself would be released from its bondage.

The mud cries out to heal again.

The seas long to obey again.

The grave aches to tremble again.

The heavens are poised to open again.

Why? Because when true sons manifest, creation finds its rhythm again. Everything in the natural longs to return to its original design, not as master, but as servant. Servant to sons. Servant to stewards. Servant to the image-bearers of God.

When Jesus walked the earth, the wind didn't argue, it obeyed. The water didn't resist, it carried Him. The tree with no fruit responded to His voice. Why? Because He wasn't just a man operating in power, He was The Son walking in identity. And when sons manifest, creation becomes still. It listens. It yields. It remembers.

"Be still," He said. And the winds hushed.

"Come forth," He said. And the grave gave up its dead.

"Peace," He declared. And storms laid down like tamed lions.

So, it is with us.

Creation doesn't need more noise. It longs for the silence that comes when sons speak. The silence of submission. The hush of recognition. The stillness of satisfaction, when creation sees the likeness of the Father again in the sons He has sent.

This is why the enemy has fought identity so viciously. If he can keep believers acting like orphans, striving like servants, and hiding like slaves, creation stays in bondage. But when sons arise, everything groans in expectation begins to sing again.

You were not just saved to escape hell.

You were born again to reveal heaven.

You were not just adopted to survive.

You were positioned to manifest.

And when you walk in your identity, everything around you aligns. Because sons do not just carry authority. They carry likeness. The world doesn't just need people who can quote Scripture. It needs people who look like the Father.

"As He is, so are we in this world." 1 John 4:17

Creation waits. Heaven watches. The earth groans.

It is time for the sons of God to rise. Not in arrogance. Not in performance. But in revealed identity.

This is the age of manifestation.

Creation waiting for sons

God isn't just restoring people to heaven; He's releasing heaven through people. Creation isn't groaning for more religion, rules, or rituals, it's longing for sons. Sons carry God's nature, voice, and authority in the earth.

"Your Kingdom come, Your will be done, on earth as it is in heaven." – Matthew 6:10

Sonship is not just believed, it's expressed

True sonship has visible fruit. Identity changes behavior. We manifest the Father when we walk in love (Ephesians 5:1–2), demonstrate authority over chaos (Mark 4:39), release peace, healing, and wisdom.

The world knows the Father by watching the sons.

"He who has seen Me has seen the Father." – John 14:9

Jesus showed us the pattern; sons reflect the Father, not themselves. When you manifest sonship, you become a mirror of heaven to the earth. Again:

"As He is, so are we in this world." – 1 John 4:17

Adam was placed in the garden to cultivate and guard (Genesis 2:15). Sons don't just host God's presence; they advance God's order. Wherever you go, sonship brings, peace to chaos, truth to confusion, restoration to ruin.

You cannot manifest what hasn't been fashioned in maturity. The difference between a believer and a son is not status, but maturity.

"Though he is a child, he differs nothing from a slave…" – Galatians 4:1

Sonship grows as we yield to the Spirit and respond to correction.

Sons carry the family name

Sons not only carry the likeness of the Father, they carry the family name.

This is why the Great Commission is more than just evangelism; it's about extension of the family. When Jesus gave the command in Matthew 28:19, *"Go therefore and make disciples of all nations, baptizing them in the name of the Father, and of the Son, and of the Holy Spirit,"* He wasn't giving a formula, He was revealing a family framework.

That name, the singular name, not plural names, is the unified identity of the family of God. One name. One household. One Spirit.

Only sons can immerse nations into the family.

Because only sons carry the family name in spirit and in truth. Servants may announce the kingdom, but only sons can extend it. Baptism is not just about symbolic water, it's about bringing people into the identity of the Father's house. Into the lineage. Into the likeness. Into the DNA. Into the name.

Sons manifest the Kingdom by making disciples, not into themselves, not into systems, but into the family of God. They don't just teach behavior, they transfer identity. They don't just preach doctrine, they reproduce nature. They don't just build ministries, they multiply sons.

Jesus did not commission us to simply multiply followers; He commissioned us to extend the Father's family. When He said, *"Go therefore and make disciples of all nations, baptizing them in the name of the Father, and of the Son, and of the Holy Spirit"* (Matthew 28:19), He was authorizing sons to bring others into the family name. This was not just a call to conversion, but a call to belonging.

Only sons can baptize others into the name of the Father, because only sons carry that name. Only sons know how to extend the household of God, not merely expand the reach of a religious institution. The commission to disciple nations is a commission to immerse them into identity, into the triune life of Father, Son, and Spirit. And this mission is deeply rooted in love, family, and sonship.

This is what Paul unveils in Ephesians 3:14–19: *"For this reason I bow my knees to the Father of our Lord Jesus Christ, from whom the whole family in heaven and earth is named, that He would grant you, according to the riches of His glory, to be strengthened with might through His Spirit in the inner man, that Christ may dwell in your hearts through faith; that you, being rooted and grounded in love, may be able to comprehend with all the saints what is the width and length and depth and height— to know the love of Christ which passes knowledge; that you may be filled with all the fullness of God."* (NKJV)

Paul's prayer is not for performance but for presence, that the inner man would be strengthened by the Spirit, that Christ would dwell, and that believers would be rooted in the Father's love. This rooting is not institutional, it is familial. Paul bows his knees to the Father, from whom the whole family in heaven and earth is named. In other words, the Great Commission is not a global business strategy. It is a family expansion mandate.

To make disciples is to bring sons into the Father's house, to immerse them in the fullness of Christ, in the love that grounds identity, and in the Spirit that seals sonship.

Sons don't just preach, they impart the family nature. They don't just declare truth, they reproduce the DNA of Heaven. Christ, the firstborn among many brethren (Romans 8:29), became the blueprint. And every true son carries not just His message but His likeness.

Ephesians 3 gives us the apostolic pattern: kneel before the Father, root sons in love, strengthen the inner man, and fill them with the fullness of God. This is how the family grows, not through strategies, but through sonship.

The Great Commission, then, is a family mandate. It is the sending forth of mature sons to awaken sonship in others. It is the call to disciple nations, not into religion, but into relationship. Into the Father's house. Into the Spirit's power. Into the Son's likeness.

This is what Jesus modeled. He was not just sent as a preacher or prophet, He was the Firstborn among many brethren (Romans 8:29). He revealed the Father so that others could become sons. He brought the Kingdom so that others could enter the house. And now, He entrusts that same mission to sons, not to employees or hired hands, but to those who know the heart of the Father and carry His name with honor.

So therefore…

"Let your light so shine before men, that they may see your good works and glorify your Father in heaven." – Matthew 5:16

Your light isn't meant to spotlight you, it's meant to glorify your Father. Sonship is not just a revelation, it's a responsibility to reflect Him well.

Reflection Questions

1. How do you view your identity in relation to the Father's name? Do you see yourself as one who carries the family name and likeness of God?

_____

_____

_____

_____

_____

2. In what ways have you approached the Great Commission, as a servant's task or a son's inheritance? How does this shift your understanding of making disciples?

_____

_____

_____

_____

_____

3. Do you believe creation can respond to your voice because you are a son? Why or why not, and what would change if you did?

_____

_____

_____

_____

4. What area of your life needs to move from merely representing God to extending Him? Where are you being invited to function in likeness, not just authority?

_____

_____

_____

_____

_____

_____

_____

_____

5. How can you more intentionally bring others into the Father's house, not just into faith, but into family? What does that look like practically in your ministry, workplace, or home?

_____

_____

_____

_____

_____

_____

_____

148

6. Have you ever tried to walk in dominion without returning to sonship first? What was the result, and what might God be inviting you back into now?

_____

_____

_____

_____

_____

_____

_____

_____

7. What part of creation around you might be 'groaning' for your sonship to manifest? Is there a sphere of influence waiting for you to rise in identity?

_____

_____

_____

_____

_____

_____

_____

NOTES

CHAPTER 10
Spiritual Sonship

I was twelve years old when my natural father passed away. Grief has a way of creating silence, but mine was interrupted the very next day as I found myself in church, broken, searching, but strangely drawn. In that moment, I surrendered my life to the Father. I didn't understand everything, but something in me knew He was waiting for me.

Years later, a prophetic word came to me: "God is going to send you a spiritual father." At the time, I didn't even know what that meant. I had heard of mentors, pastors, and leaders, but "spiritual father" felt like a foreign phrase. Still, it lingered in my heart like a seed awaiting its soil.

The day came unexpectedly. I was preaching at a conference, and afterward, a man named Bishop Gary Clowers sat down with me and began to speak. But it wasn't just his words I heard, it was his voice. There was a weight, a depth, a familiarity that stirred something in me. I had never heard his voice before, yet I knew it. I heard the voice of a father.

That was over twenty-five years ago, and since then I've not just walked beside him, I've been fathered by him. I've watched his life. I've grown through his example. His preaching has been powerful, but his presence has taught me more than any sermon. He has shown me what it looks like to live in the integrity of spiritual sonship, and in doing so, he's helped awaken the same in me.

This is what Paul meant when he wrote to the Corinthians: *"Though you have ten thousand instructors in Christ, yet you do not have many fathers"* (1 Corinthians 4:15).

Paul was not dismissing the role of teachers, he was elevating the necessity of fathers. Teachers inform, but fathers transform. Teachers pass on what they've learned. Fathers impart who they are. Teachers can fill a pulpit. But fathers fill a life. Teachers can give you knowledge. But fathers impart who they are.

And in the Kingdom, we need both. But too many have been satisfied with information, while starving for impartation.

Paul didn't just teach Timothy and Titus, he begot them. *"To Timothy, my true son in the faith…"* he writes. To Titus, *"my own son after the common faith."* These were not professional relationships built on shared ministry goals. These were sacred bonds, birthed in spiritual intimacy and sealed through consistent impartation. He says they were begotten by his gospel, not just a message, but a way of life entrusted and embodied.

Many have entered ministry through inspiration. But true sons are begotten through impartation.

Paul didn't just raise up churches; he raised up sons.

Timothy, Titus, Onesimus, these were more than ministry associates. They were spiritual sons. Paul wrote of Timothy, *"I have no one like-minded"* (Phil. 2:20), and to Titus he wrote, *"my true son in our common faith"* (Titus 1:4). These weren't honorary titles, they were relational realities. They lived in Paul's heart, not just his itinerary.

When Paul says, *"I have begotten you through the gospel,"* he's speaking of more than conversion. He's referring to a gospel that gives birth to sons, not just church members. And this gospel, the gospel of the Kingdom, is not about assembling congregations, but establishing households.

Spiritual sonship is more than mentorship. It is a covenant relationship where identity is affirmed, character is shaped, and legacy is forged. And like all true sonship, it begins with recognizing the Father's voice, even if it comes through the mouth of a man. Again, Paul's language in 1 Corinthians 4:15 is piercing: *"You have ten thousand instructors in Christ, but not many fathers."*

The word "instructors" in the Greek is paidagōgos, a word that referred to a guardian, a tutor, a disciplinary guide. These were servants assigned to train up children, (likened to a modern day nanny or babysitter), often through rigid oversight. They could correct behavior, enforce lessons, and regulate development. But they were not fathers. They had no power to give identity, no authority to release inheritance, and no personal investment in the destiny of the child. They were keepers of rules, not carriers of love.

In contrast, Paul declares, *"I have begotten you through the gospel."* He wasn't merely a theological voice in their life, he was a spiritual parent. He didn't just teach them doctrine, he imparted identity. And he did it through his gospel. That's not arrogance. It's apostolic confidence. Paul had received something so real from Christ that it birthed sons, not just students. It wasn't a message he borrowed, it was a life he carried. And that gospel didn't just call people to faith; it called them into family.

Timothy was one of those sons. Paul writes to the Philippians: *"But you know his proven character, that as a son with his father he served with me in the gospel"* Phil. 2:22.

Notice, Timothy didn't serve Paul. He served with him. There was no hierarchy of exploitation. This wasn't about using young men for ministry leverage. This was a father-son dynamic that empowered Timothy to grow, to lead, and to eventually pastor the church at Ephesus.

This is the model of spiritual sonship.

It's not top-down control, it's bottom-up cultivation. True spiritual fathers don't build platforms on the backs of sons. They build sons who will one day surpass them. They don't stunt development for their own legacy, they plant deeply so that legacy can continue without them.

In today's church culture, we've often seen giftedness exalted above fathering. We've seen charisma without character, ministry without covering, and talent without tethering. And we've called it success. But without fathers, we produce orphans, highly skilled but emotionally adrift. Anointed but unaccountable. Sent but not safe.

Paul tells the Corinthians, *"Imitate me, as I imitate Christ"* (1 Cor. 11:1). This is spiritual fathering: a life worthy of imitation. Paul didn't offer perfection, but he offered presence. He didn't just correct, he connected. He walked with his sons. He warned them with tears. He gave his life for the sake of the churches and those he birthed in the Spirit.

154

This is what I've come to understand from walking with my spiritual father. Watching his consistency. Witnessing how he handled conflict, betrayal, pressure, and blessing. I didn't just learn how to preach, I learned how to stand. I didn't just learn ministry, I learned manhood. And that came not from classroom lectures, but from a life lived in front of me.

That's the difference between teachers and fathers.

A teacher points you to principles.

A father forms you with presence.

A teacher shows you how to serve God.

A father shows you what it means to be a son.

A teacher prepares you for ministry.

A father prepares you for legacy.

The platform without "paternity"

There's a tragedy that happens when someone desires the platform of ministry without submitting to the process of sonship. They may hunger for influence, for authority, even for spiritual inheritance, but they bypass the identity needed to carry it well. This results in instability. Just like the younger son in the parable of Luke 15, who demanded the portion of goods without understanding the heart of the father, these individuals will eventually waste what they prematurely possess.

Ministry can never replace maturity. And promotion apart from process breeds pride. A spiritual son receives correction without rebellion, walks in accountability without fear, and stays faithful even when unseen. Sons understand that submission is not weakness, it's security. They don't chase stages, they follow fathers.

The danger of bypassing sonship is that you may inherit something you're not equipped to steward. Without the heart of a son, you'll end up using people to build your kingdom instead of building people for God's.

Spiritual fathers heal orphan mentalities

Spiritual fathering is more than mentorship, it's healing. Many believers carry orphan wounds from natural families, church hurt, or deep rejection. They don't know how to trust, how to be received, or how to rest in identity. They serve tirelessly trying to earn love they already have access to.

A true spiritual father steps into that ache, not to take advantage of it, but to bring healing to it. Like Paul with the Corinthians, a father says: *"I didn't come to condemn you, I came to call you into identity."*

When a father is present, sons begin to believe:

- I can be corrected and still be loved.
- I can fail and not be discarded.
- I can be seen and still be safe.

It is this dynamic, love that affirms without enabling, and correction that restores without wounding, that transforms spiritual orphans into mature sons.

Sonship creates safe spaces for growth and maturity

The spiritual house becomes a greenhouse when fathers are in place. It's not a place of perfection, it's a place of process. Sons aren't afraid to ask questions, to confess weakness, or to admit they're still becoming. Why? Because love removes fear.

I remember times when I didn't know what to do. But I knew where to go. My father in the Lord didn't just have answers, he had patience. He gave space for me to grow without shaming me for being in process. That's what fathers do. They hold space so sons can become.

This is why Paul uses the word nurture (1 Thess. 2:7) when describing how he related to the church. The spiritual family is not a corporate ladder, it's a covenant environment. Sons don't compete, they complement. And fathers don't crush, they cultivate.

Inheritance isn't a position, it's a portion

Too often, we associate spiritual inheritance with titles, pulpits, or ministry roles. But Paul's relationship with Timothy and Titus was not built on platforms, it was built on impartation. He didn't just say *"Take my place."* He said, *"Carry my heart."*

True sons receive a portion, not just a position. Elijah threw his mantle on Elisha, but the greater inheritance came through years of walking together. Watching. Serving. Learning. Honoring.

When sons are faithful, a portion of their father's spirit rests on them (see Numbers 11:17; 2 Kings 2:9–10). That's legacy. It's not what you're handed in a moment, it's what you carry after years of alignment.

Receive, walk, and become

Sonship is not a theological term, it's a transformational reality. You don't just learn about it. You live it.

If you've never had a spiritual father, pray for one. And while you wait, let the Holy Spirit begin to show you the Father's heart in a deeper way. You will not fully understand how to be a spiritual son to man until you become a secure son to God. However, having a spiritual father, will aid you in grasping sonship to God.

If you've been wounded by poor examples, let healing begin. God didn't abandon the model of spiritual family just because some misrepresented it.

Jesus still gives the lonely a family. And He still places the orphan in a house.

If you are a spiritual father, live the life worthy of imitation. Be more than a voice, be a life that speaks.

If you are a son, be faithful, be formed, and be fruitful. The day will come when you too will be entrusted with sons. What you model today is what they will manifest tomorrow.

Reflection Questions

1. Have you ever longed for a spiritual platform without submitting to spiritual fathering?

_____

_____

_____

_____

_____

2. Who has fathered you in the Lord? Whether they are distant or close, known or unknown—what fruit has come from their presence (or absence) in your life?

_____

_____

_____

_____

_____

_____

3. Do you struggle to receive correction as a sign of love?

_____

_____

_____

_____

_____

4. Can you identify orphan tendencies in your walk with God or others? Do you battle with needing approval, fearing rejection, or equating your worth with your service?

_____

_____

_____

_____

_____

_____

5. Are you more comfortable serving than being received?

_____

_____

_____

_____

6. Has your view of inheritance been shaped by titles, roles, or ministry influence? How can you begin to pursue the portion of the Father's heart instead of just a position?

_____

_____

_____

_____

_____

_____

7. What has your spiritual formation taught you about being a son? Are there moments where you received love, identity, or correction that shaped who you are?

_____

_____

_____

_____

_____

_____

_____

_____

8. If you are fathering others—what are they inheriting from you? Is your life a model that could be imitated, not just your message?

_____

_____

_____

_____

_____

_____

_____

9. Are you asking God to send a spiritual father—or have you asked Him to make you one? What does your journey of sonship prepare you to impart?

_____

_____

_____

_____

_____

_____

_____

_____

10. What is one practical step you can take this week to live more securely as a son? (e.g., scheduling time with a mentor, releasing resentment, or resting without guilt.)

_____

_____

_____

_____

_____

_____

_____

_____

NOTES

CONCLUSION:
THE RISE OF SONS

From the dust of creation to the revelation of redemption, God's intent has never changed: He is building a family of sons who bear His image, carry His name, and reveal His glory.

This journey, from orphans to heirs, from performance to presence, from servants to sons, is not about status alone. It is about likeness. It is about intimacy. And ultimately, it is about inheritance. You were never meant to serve from fear but to reign from love.

The Kingdom of God is not built on giftedness, charisma, or religious performance. It is built on relationship with the Father, secured through Christ, and revealed by the Spirit of adoption.

As you close this book, the invitation remains open, step into your place, live as a son, raise others with a father's heart, and let creation see the Father by watching you.

"As He is, so are we in this world." – 1 John 4:17 (NKJV)

Let the rise of sons begin, one healed heart, one faithful house, one legacy at a time.

AFTERWORD

The cry for identity in the body of Christ trumpets through the barrenness of our emptiness. As I reflect on the spirit within these pages, it becomes clear that there's a vital element missing and much that is lacking in our walk with God. In the silence of our isolation, we hear the call of becoming, the call back to sonship where we have disconnected from the source, called Father, leaving us orphans, to get back to the Father's table and not just the fields of performance.

The contents of this exegesis on sonship comes with waves of impartation as you allow the Spirit to wash over you through each page. This is not just informative but transformative and will "Restore your dignity, Reframe your calling and Release your legacy" (Apostle Chris Turney)

A dissecting of the Orphan spirit was such a blessing as Apostle Chris identified key issues, root causes and kingdom cures. The remedy is found in understanding the Spirit of adoption which restores the sound that was lost in Eden, the sound of sons walking confidently in the presence of the Father. Those affected and hurt by inaccurate representation of father will find healing and refreshing at the realignment with the accurate purpose and intention God had for us from the beginning. In the layers of this masterpiece lies the very DNA of the patterned Firstborn Son, the image of the Father.

In our pursuit for present day truth, we ultimately have to open ourselves to collide heart to heart, past the hurt and disappointment, past the distrust and rejection. The fibre of relationship interwoven in the father and son merger blends the fragrances of honour, trust, patience and yielded-ness to create an incense from the altar of obedience. In becoming, that brings complete healing and resurrection to what God intended.

I took time to read and re-read every page, to mine out the nuggets of truth, keys which unlock chambers closed up for many years and allow the healing waters of truth to just wash me. The gems locked up in the parable of the prodigal son revealing our orphan mentality and performance mindset made me see sonship in a new light.

May God find the image and likeness of son, which He predestined ordained from the first breath of creation in us in complete measure and maturity at the climax of the ages.

Riaan du Toit
Transforming Your World Ministries

www.ingramcontent.com/pod-product-compliance
Lightning Source LLC
Chambersburg PA
CBHW071104280326
41928CB00051B/2808